FIGURES IN
MODERN LITERATURE

Figures in Modern Literature

By

J. B. Priestley

London: John Lane The Bodley Head Limited
New York: Dodd, Mead and Company

First published . *June 1924*
Reprinted . . . *Dec. 1924*

Made and printed in Great Britain at
The Mayflower Press, Plymouth. William Brendon & Son, Ltd.

CONTENTS

NOTE.—*All these papers, with the exception of those on Mr. Santayana and Mr. Squire, have appeared in the* London Mercury, *and I take this opportunity of thanking the editor for his hospitality. It must not be understood that I necessarily consider these figures the most important in contemporary literature, but I do hold that they all are important, and I can only hope that they will prove a welcome change from the usual set, the Shaw–Wells–Galsworthy–Chesterton gallery that is now so familiar, particularly as some of my authors have not been treated at any length before. I can only hope too that such authors will not find my voice so unpleasant that they would have preferred an unbroken silence.—J. B. P.*

FIGURES IN
MODERN LITERATURE

FIGURES IN MODERN LITERATURE

MR. ARNOLD BENNETT

THERE are more than fifty volumes now in the " List of Works to date," that faces the title-page of every book by Mr. Bennett, and at the very sight of this monstrous bibliography a kind of despair falls upon the critic who would try to estimate such an author. Nor is there any way out of it ; the list must be faced resolutely, manfully, or the criticism will suffer. It will not do to treat Mr. Bennett as the author of only three books instead of fifty-three ; we cannot write at length about *The Old Wives' Tale*, *Clayhanger*, and, let us say, *Riceyman Steps*, and then condemn all our author's other works, his fantasias, short stories, plays, pocket philosophies and books of travel and chit-chat, to the pulping machines with one wave of the hand. Many of these works may cut a better figure in their author's ledger accounts than they ever will in the literary histories of our time, but they are there and cannot be rightly ignored, for the real Mr. Bennett is not the writer of this or that book, but is to be found somewhere behind all these books, perhaps buried beneath them, but buried alive. Moreover, it is dangerous to dismiss whole rows of these less important volumes, because Mr. Bennett, being amazingly unequal, can suddenly fall to writing well in unexpected places just as he can fall to writing badly. As examples of the craft of writing, the actual business of setting down a number of facts and impressions in words, as distinct from the wider art of creation in literature, he has probably given us nothing better than the first few sketches in *Paris Nights*, which was called a " bold, brilliant, exciting book " when it first came out, but has not, I imagine, attracted much attention recently ; so that, to take only this one example, Mr. Bennett cannot be fairly judged without his *Paris Nights*. It is clear that to be seen distinctly he must be seen against the background of his complete works, good, bad, and indifferent ; many people only know the author of *The Human Machine* or *How To Make the Best of Life*, some others only know the author of *The Old Wives' Tale* or *Clayhanger*, but both authors must be the subjects of any critical estimate of Mr. Arnold Bennett. The only danger there is in such a thorough examination, when space is limited, is that the mere bulk of work prevents close detailed criticism, with its eye on the individual book, its insistence upon chapter and verse, and inevitably encourages that loose easy generalizing mode of criticism of which Mr. Bennett so far has had, perhaps, more than his fair share. This danger, however, is the least of many, and if Mr. Bennett has to suffer yet a few more easy generalizations, he must remember that he himself has been generalizing no less easily and loosely throughout some half a hundred volumes.

These volumes are the work of a trinity of authors. The first, the most prolific and easily the best known, is the omniscient Mr. Bennett, the connoisseur, the tipster of life and the arts, the man who can put you wise, who can tell you a thing or two, who has made a stir in the big city and is now " in the swim," " in the movement " (his favourite phrases—see works *passim*), a terrible fellow who knows more about life than even the head waiter of the Grand Babylon Hotel. He has been everywhere and knows everything ; he is curious and knowledgeable about cities, books, railway trains, soup, water-colours, frocks and skirts, the Parisian Theatre, making tea, opera, and barbers ; he goes through life and the arts like a profiteer refurnishing the house, demanding only " the best of everything " ; he is a lover of experts and probably wishes to become the expert of experts. In all this intense curiosity about every side of the life of his own time there is a zest, gusto, infectious enthusiasm, that is entirely admirable. At a time when so many clever persons are trying, in one way or another, to escape from life, to pretend that the real world is not there, we have here a very clever man who cannot have too much of it, a realist who discovers as much delight in a fact as some of his fellow-authors do in an idea, and has the power to communicate something of that delight. Whatever else he may be, this Mr. Bennett is certainly a great journalist. Yet the result of this intense curiosity, this unflagging zest for things, is an attitude that is knowing rather than wise. There are too many limitations. Whole sides of life and states of mind, and these by no means the least important, some of them perhaps the most important, seem to mean nothing to him ; he knows his world like the great journalist he is, but it is still the journalist's world, the world of the evening papers and not that of the poets, the saints and mystics, the great philosophers and historians ; the voice is always that of an oracle, brimmed with certainties, but it is too often the oracle of the smoke-room, the cleverest bagman in the hotel, who knows a thing or two about Women and Good Cigars. Knowledge may make for confidence, but it is usually left behind in the race by cheerful ignorance, and this Mr. Bennett (there are two others), having left off thinking deeply and feeling sensitively at a very early age, very quickly became completely confident, so that the section of his work which, with something like blasphemy, he cheerfully labels " Belles-Lettres " is nothing less than an epic of the cocksure. In his so-called Pocket Philosophies, or at least in some of them, he combines the vulgarity of the early Utilitarians (whose detachment perhaps modified it) with the equal vulgarity of a typical smart young materialist of the 'Eighties, whose dying whispers can be caught in Mr. Bennett's favourite metaphors, his talk about the Human Machine and so forth. Many sensitive readers, after learning from our author how to make the best of life, must have come to the conclusion that life was not worth making the best of, so sadly had it been vulgarized. So, too, his criticism, though there are delightful elements in it, is too often merely the cheerful impudence of a clever man who is not making a critical effort and is too interested either in attacking or following literary fashions to be capable of making such an effort. It is this Mr. Bennett who would take away the pen from one of the others in order to insert a reference to a fashionably obscure French composer or painter in a short story of the Five Towns ; such references, though they played little part in the stories, did at least show that the writer himself was " in the movement." And it is this first Mr. Bennett who is responsible for the miscellaneous books, who contributes a paragraph on every other page in the lighter novels, does his share of the dialogue in the plays, and even finds his way into the more serious novels. Unfortunately for him and fortunately for us, however, his work, except that in the Pocket Philosophies, is usually brought to nothing because there is some one at hand to give the game away, to reveal the fact that the writer is not really a bored encyclopædic guide to the life of wealth and taste, but is really a dazed enthusiast, a kind of wondering poet from the provinces, staggered at the way he is " getting on." You have only to open the first book to hand of Mr. Bennett's to see how frankly the game is given away : " Then it suddenly occurred to me that if I had gambled with

B

louis instead of five-franc pieces I should have made 200 francs—200 francs in rather over an hour ! Oh, luxury ! Oh, being-in-the-swim ! Oh, smartness ! Oh, gilded and delicious sin ! " That is not the first Mr. Bennett at all ; it is the second, chanting his happy litany.

This second Mr. Bennett is simpler, more naïve and enthusiastic, and altogether more engaging than the first ; and he is nearer by a thousand leagues to the soul of literature, for he has one quality that is an essential ingredient of great romance—a sense of wonder. True, it is very limited ; not only is the past closed to it, that living past which has been woven into the fabric of tradition and has secured for our delight the fragrance, colour, and bloom of centuries, but much else that does not glitter on the surface of things is hidden from it too ; and yet even this limitation is our gain, for it means that our author is lost in wonder at things that most other authors have ceased to wonder at, so that in his own fashion he has created a new kind of poetry. He is Wonder in a billy-cock, Romance with an excursion ticket to London, as mazed and dizzy at the sight of Harrods or the Savoy Hotel as Mr. de la Mare is with his dream of Arabia ; he comes to a metropolitan hotel as Childe Roland came to the Dark Tower. The advantages of being a provincial, one who has long been acquainted with the solid realities of life as they are to be discovered in small industrial towns, where the solid realities are most starkly displayed, and who is now zestful and ripe for the magnificent frivolities, the splendid mummeries, of London, these advantages were never better illustrated. In novel after novel, particularly those of the lighter kind, it is this Mr. Bennett, with his fresh vision, his humour and high spirits, who carries off the situation ; he has only to take us into a big hotel or restaurant or the Turkish Baths, and the trick is done and we are all excited, interested or amused again, all stepping out of King's Cross or St. Pancras still grasping the return half of our tickets, trying to look like persons who know what is what and are not to be trifled with, great city or no great city, but inwardly out-gasping and gaping stout Cortez himself. He does it time after time ; Denry's whole existence, as we know him in *The Card* and *The Regent*, is one long excited climb ; Priam Farll and his lady go trotting about the town and we are thrilled anew with them ; Mr. Prohack quits his office to be one of the idle rich and has some wonderful sensations in the West End ; and so on and so forth ; the situation never palls on the writer and we catch something of his zest. He is the rhapsodist of gigantic hotels and restaurants, White Cities, fashionable theatres and clubs, Turkish Baths, two thousand pound motor-cars, pianolas, exclusive tailors, labour-saving devices, everything that is modern, expensive, luxurious, and not to be found in the Five Towns, or at least, in the Five Towns when Mr. Bennett lived there. Practically all his lighter stories, most of which he certainly enjoyed writing, are stories of wealth and luxury ; they are crowded with millionaires who live in suites at colossal hotels, and are, in reality, a kind of fairy story that Mr. Bennett, seeking relaxation after the austerities of naturalistic fiction, is telling to himself, an old dream that comes back to his mind every time he sits down to write an easy idle tale. There is a fairy tale somewhere in every creative artist, and Mr. Bennett's is an up-to-date medley of millionaires whose hotel bills are twenty-five to fifty pounds a day, magnificently expensive and charming women of the world, experts, from medical to sartorial, ready at any moment to dance attendance and charge astounding fees, a full chorus of chefs, waiters, chauffeurs, and flunkeys; and in the midst of it all some half-sophisticated, half-simple soul, busy fulfilling old dreams and pinching himself to discover if he is yet awake; while in the background, the symbol of the luxurious life, the heaven of all climbers and Cards and Human Machines and men who live on twenty-four hours a day, there looms and blazes against the night sky—the Grand Babylon Hotel. If Mr. Bennett should ever become a legend and his work come to be regarded as a number of folk tales (and stranger things have happened), about one-third of his works will be grouped together as the Grand Babylon Hotel Cycle and attempts will no doubt be made to determine its religious significance. Meanwhile, the significance for us of these comedies of high life and high jinks that are played, without regard to expense, on carpets five inches thick, lies in the fact that in them the dreams and aspirations, the romantic possibilities of what had hitherto appeared to be the least promising class in the kingdom, the middle-aged members of the middle-class, have been seized upon and pressed into service as they never have before, for the possible instruction of a few sociologists and the delight of all good novel readers. Finally, the secret of these romantic comedies of middle-age by a middle-aged novelist, the secret of their somewhat naïve charm, is that at heart they are simply boyish ; this second Mr. Bennett is nothing more (nor less) than a brilliant and delightful youth, not quite out of his teens, who has outgrown his tin soldiers and treasure islands only to make the Grand Babylon Hotel, golden, shining, the centre of his dreams and summit of his aspirations.

But even though another ten stories should be added to it, the Grand Babylon Hotel cannot entirely blot out the night sky and the strange stars, and not all the hosts of porters and page boys can prevent Change and Death from forcing their way into its velvet, gilded lounge ; in short, there is a great deal more in life, and in the art that would pretend to grapple with life, than was ever dreamed of in the philosophy of the second Mr. Bennett. But there is yet another Mr. Bennett, the third and last, who has made the largest contribution to the major works but who is yet less distinct than the others and can hardly be described, without grave injustice, in a few lines. He does not glide over the surface of things as the other two do ; he has not their almost metallic optimism ; indeed, all his brave epicurean gestures cannot prevent us from noticing that he is at heart troubled and somewhat pitiful, sceptical, but, despite his fine show of indifference, not coolly sceptical, but disturbed, leaning ever towards pessimism. He it is who has written so many passages like the following, which comes from that little encounter between Carlotta and old Lord Alcar in *Sacred and Profane Love*:

" . . . . Only the fool and the very young expect happiness. The wise merely hope to be interested, at least not to be bored, in their passage through the world. Nothing is so interesting as love and grief and the one involves the other. Ah! would I not do the same again!"

He spoke gravely, wistfully, and vehemently, as if employing the last spark of divine fire that was left in his decrepit frame. This undaunted confession of a faith which had survived twenty years of inactive meditation, this banner waved by an expiring arm in the face of the eternity that mocks at the transience of human beings, filled me with admiration. . . .

He it was—to go from an early book to one of the most recent—who wrote the title (but nothing else) of the last volume of philosophy for the million that the first, the omniscient, Mr. Bennett gave us; the title is *How to Make the Best of Life*, which has a strange ring, suggesting that the writer, so apparently cheerful, so cocksure, believes in his heart of hearts that life is a bad business—but (and we can see him yawning and shrugging) he can give the young readers a few tips that might ease their gradual descent into the grave. He it was, too, who devised that fine melancholy thing, *The Old Wives' Tale*, which has two suffering heroines, Constance and Sophia Baines, and three conquering heroes, Time,

Mutability, and Death. The shadows of these three are over *Clayhanger* too, and here again we cannot fail to notice how, in selecting and arranging his material, he has chosen to emphasize the passing of the old, the coming of the new, change and decay. Here, we feel that life, which may be something more than sound and fury, may be coloured with passion, shot through with beauty, brought into harmony for an hour or so by love, is still a tale told by an idiot or the silliest, saddest old wife. Many critics have seen in this Mr. Bennett a sociologist, mainly because sociology in the guise of fiction has been fashionable and Mr. Bennett happens to have worked closely over large canvases and has been inspired more by the character of a whole region than by a few individuals ; but actually, though he has sometimes taken over a few sociological tricks from his friend, Mr. Wells, he is no sociologist. Like Mr. Wells, he is fond of emphasizing the fact that times change, and passages like this are common :

John Baines had belonged to the past, to the age when men really did think of their souls, when orators by phrases could move crowds to fury or to pity, when no one had learnt to hurry, when Demos was only turning in his sleep, when the sole beauty of life resided in its inflexible and slow dignity, when hell really had no bottom and a gilt-clasped Bible really was the secret of England's greatness. Mid-Victorian England lay sleeping on that mahogany bed. Ideals had passed away with John Baines. It is thus that ideals die ; not in the conventional pageantry of honoured death, but sorrily, ignobly, while one's head is turned. . . .

and he will often show a whole country-side moving

from one era to another, but unlike Mr. Wells (with his laboratory and lecture-room manner), he does not describe growth and development, movement towards a certain end, so much as simply change itself, the social kaleidoscope. As for his pessimism, his vaguely uneasy scepticism, that is always liable to show itself when the easy mental attitudes of the omniscient and the wondering Mr. Bennett can no longer be maintained, it is rather felt everywhere, like an atmosphere, than definitely encountered; but it is certainly there, and it is this that makes so many persons, men and women who do not ask for barley-sugar from literature, who can relish their Hardy, Meredith, Conrad, indifferent or even antagonistic to Mr. Bennett's finest work; and even the rest of us must have caught ourselves and our friends more often heartily praising such work than returning to it for another reading. Mr. Bennett's literary methods, as distinct from his attitude of mind, have, of course, their influence here, and they will be noticed below; but it is worth remarking that this third Mr. Bennett, like the two others, though in a less degree, has still some unfortunate limitations. We feel a want of values, and notice a certain insensitiveness to the finer shades of feeling, the more subtle traits of character, the more poetical and mystical states of mind; but in addition, in these major works, so rich and marvellously well contrived, he has brought us so far, given us so much of life, that we ask to be taken a little further, to be given a little more, and we ask in vain; and that

which is usually lacking, the want of which sometimes makes us turn away from some of the best story-
telling of our time, is something that is essential in
a work of art on any considerable scale, namely,
philosophic imagination, a quality of mind that is
present, at their best, in Hardy, Meredith, Conrad,
but only feebly represented even in Mr. Bennett's
greatest work. It is this quality that can make a
scene in a farm-kitchen an affair of the Gods and the
Titans and yet still a scene in a farm-kitchen ; the
shadows of its protagonists are thrown upon the
sky, and there is no end to the significance of its
actions, whole worlds are at stake. I only find a hint
of this in both *The Old Wives' Tale* or *Clayhanger ;*
there is perhaps more of it in the only novel written
since that can be compared with them, in *Riceyman
Steps*, in which we discover a drive of passions and a
tangle of loyalties that are more closely knit and
more finely presented than they are elsewhere in our
author's work. He deliberately makes all his figures
smaller than himself so that he can see round them
rather than enter into them. He is something more
than an ironical spectator ; he is frequently moved
both by a generous enthusiasm and by pity, and he
can often strike out a gushing spring of romance and
beauty from what would appear barren rock. There
is, for example, one chapter in *Clayhanger*, a chapter
that may possibly make a stronger appeal to North-
country readers than to others, which describes how
the young Clayhanger, in search of a customer of
his father's, attends a Free-and-Easy at the local

tavern and there discovers the art of clog-dancing as understood by Florence Simcox :

> Her style was not that of a male clog-dancer, but it was indubitably clog-dancing, full of marvels to the connoisseur, and to the profane naught but a highly complicated series of wooden noises. Florence's face began to perspire. Then the concertina ceased playing—so that an undistracted attention might be given to the supremely difficult final figure of the dance.
>
> And thus was rendered back to the people in the charming form of beauty that which the instincts of the artist had taken from the sordid ugliness of the people. The clog, the very emblem of the servitude and the squalor of brutalized populations, was changed, on the light feet of this favourite, into the medium of grace. Few of these men but at some time of their lives had worn the clog, had clattered in it through winter's slush, and through the freezing darkness before dawn, to the manufactory and the mill and the mine, whence after a day of labour under discipline more than military, they had clattered back to their little candle-lighted homes. One of the slatterns behind the door actually stood in clogs to watch the dancer. The clog meant everything that was harsh, foul, and desolating ; it summoned images of misery and disgust. Yet on those feet that had never worn it seriously, it became the magic instrument of pleasure, waking dulled wits and forgotten aspirations, putting upon everybody an enchantment. . . .

But if we turn back to the fifty-odd volumes, the Bennett canon, we may choose to see them not as the work of three different authors, but as the work of one author, who has been played upon by three different sets of influences corresponding to the three divisions into which his life, during its most formative period, very easily falls. There is, first, his childhood, education, and early manhood in the Five Towns. From 1867 to the beginning of the 'Nineties, young

E. A. Bennett, brisk as a bee, was unconsciously hiving facts and impressions, scenes and characters for the day when Arnold Bennett, already a smart journalist with a story or two to his credit, should seek a new element for his fiction and suddenly pluck out these fat golden honeycombs. Mr. Bennett created the Five Towns, but only after they had created him. It must not be thought, though, that he owes his success to the interest and appeal of his chosen "locality"—as some smaller writers do—for the result would have been just the same had he been born and bred in Lancashire or the West Riding, on the Tyne or the Clyde. He was made by the Five Towns only because they stuffed his head with material to which he had only (it is a big "only") to apply his later dexterity and craft to transform into magnificent fiction; and this material was so plentiful, his early memories crowded so thick and fast upon him, that his work willy-nilly took on that fullness and richness which is one of the glories of English fiction. There was a time when Mr. Bennett, under French influences, was probably all in favour of thin, rigid, brittle narratives, of the kind that are quite wrongly regarded as masterpieces of technique, and so was all against such fullness and richness, such lively and crowded canvases, but fortunately there was a divinity that shaped his ends and that divinity was the Five Towns, "smouldering and glittering" in his memory. His real mastery and his real popularity began with the Five Towns stories, and, with the exception of his latest novel, *Riceyman Steps*, all his best work is linked up with his birthplace. It must not be forgotten, too, that his early popularity was due in part to the fact that he had what we might call a " locality " reference that helped the ordinary reader to remember his name and work ; he was the Arnold Bennett who wrote amusing stories about the Five Towns. At first, in his volumes of short tales, like the *Grim Smile of the Five Towns*, and such things as *Helen with the High Hand*, he had a tendency to act the showman instead of the plain chronicler ; in the middle of a story he would beat a big drum and invite the reader to walk up, walk up, to see the strange characteristics of the Five Towns. This trick, however, in its most aggressive form, he soon dropped and there is little of it after 1908. He shares with his sturdy fellow-townsmen, whom he has described with such gusto, many leading traits, not the least of which is a robust sense of humour that, if it lacks subtlety, has at least few blind spots. Like them, too, he is always steadily aware of the grim realities, the unpleasant facts of existence ; he knows the provincial and industrial tragi-comedy. Some of the characteristics, already noted, of the omniscient Mr. Bennett can be traced back to this period. We know, from his own account, that after successfully passing the London Matriculation Examination, a very creditable performance involving a knowledge of two languages, he proceeded to educate himself and has been doing so ever since. The result is that he has hardly ever been able to relax from the awful standard of the London Matriculation; had he gone to one of our older universities he could have relaxed, as so many of us have done, into genial idling, comforted by the thought that at least he was idling at an ancient seat of learning; but having had to walk in the shadow of that unpleasantly efficient Matriculation and having been his own lecturer and director of studies, he has never been able to take knowledge easily and lightly, and so has often combined, insufferably, the learned arrogance of the expert with the aggressive knowing manner of the provincial. Fortunately, a sense of humour and a refreshing habit of candour have always stepped in to save him from the worst excesses.

The second period is that of his early years in London, when he was engaged in journalism and ingenious pot-boiling of various kinds. He became a very successful journalist, and has remained one ever since; most of his lighter novels, whatever else they may be, are certainly good journalism, and so too are many of his plays; their style and manner are often those of the short articles on the leader page of a newspaper, and their topics are frequently the topics of the moment, though not so ephemeral in interest that the novels cannot be read or the plays performed after the lapse of a few years. Such a novel as *Mr. Prohack*, for example, has only a slight story, but is such excellent journalism that it could have been split into fragments, with only a few changes, and published in this periodical and that magazine as sketches of the times. During this period he edited a popular paper for women, and it is often claimed that this experience, obviously a very valuable one, initiated him into all the secrets of feminine psychology; he was admitted behind the scenes and has stayed there ever since. Certainly no modern novelist (if we may believe women themselves) can touch in the details of a woman's life so lightly and surely; but a good deal more than a few years' acquaintance with popular journalism for women is needed to make a man the father of great daughters in literature, and if there is an advantage in knowing some feminine characteristics, as it were, off by heart, such easy knowledge is also not without danger to a creative artist, as we shall presently see. What such popular journalism did do was to give him a thorough understanding and appreciation of the topics, the situations, incidents, and characters that have the firmest hold upon the popular imagination; and this understanding enabled him to lead the monster gently by the nose, and taught him not to fly in its face. His journalism gave him ideas, not purely literary ideas, but ideas of every description, and no novelist of our time has had more. With him, as the late Dixon Scott once pointed out, there is no deception; he not only tells us exactly what his characters can do, but he actually shows us how they do it; when he introduces into a novel a new kind of house or an ideal theatre he gives us an exact description of the labour-saving devices in the house and the interior arrangements of the theatre; when he tells us how Denry made a fortune and a reputation as a wit and joker, a Card, we see exactly how it was done, we are given the schemes, the wit and jokes, until we realize that the writer himself is a Card too, and that we might all set up as Cards if we studied the life of Denry with sufficient care. Further, it taught him that the great sin in writing is to be dull, and since then he has been many things, exasperating, irritating, intolerable, but never dull ; even when he was working under the influence of the bleakest naturalistic theory of the art of fiction, he was never dull, but always bright, alert, efficient. But while he learned to see the dramatic situation, and the equally dramatic " problem " in his miscellaneous writing, and to make his style snappy and perky and button-holing, in all but his very best pieces of work we see the trail of the newspaper and the bright weekly all over his situations and his style, and in the latter we too often hear the click and rattle of efficient mechanism that is functioning freely (the metaphor and the several words that compose it are all favourites of Mr. Bennett's) rather than the music of an instrument, finely tuned and delicately handled. Even in his best things he never achieves a really fine style. He has written a good deal about prose style, but it is very doubtful if he realizes what is involved in a great prose style. He, in common with many other writers on the subject, appears to think that style is simply the accurate expression of the writer's matter or thought. But style, in the purely literary sense of the term, has a threefold function : it expresses the thought by a logical arrangement of symbols ; it contrives to intensify emotion by its undertones and overtones, suggestion and association of all kinds ; and further it gives pleasure of itself merely as an arrangement, a pattern, a decoration. Most of us think ourselves fortunate if we succeed in making our style fulfil the first part of its function, and Mr. Bennett, like Mr. Wells, but unlike Mr. Hardy or Mr. Conrad, is no more successful. He sometimes comes near to a personal style by making use of certain tricks, the chief of which is a succession of short exclamatory sentences that begin with a panting conjunction and end with a gasping mark of exclamation ; but the tricks are far from being pleasant. Indeed, had there not been another set of influences at work, Mr. Bennett might have declined altogether into a writer of bright melodramas and amusing clap-trap articles. "When one looks back," he has written, "one sees that certain threads run through one's life, making a sort of pattern in it. These threads and the nature of the pattern are not perceived until long after the events constituting them. I now see that there has been a French thread through my life." This last set of influences, in short, is the result of his early interest in French, chiefly modern French literature (at a time when his acquaintance with our own literature was only slight), and of an equal interest in French life that finally led to his living in France for nearly ten years.

It is obvious that an impressionable man of letters cannot prefer a foreign literature (and one entirely alien in its outlook and manner) and suffer a voluntary exile for so long without some considerable change taking place in his point of view and his methods of work. Only a long and close study, based on something more than an outside knowledge of Mr. Bennett's work, could assess the value of such influences, but we may reasonably permit ourselves a few guesses. In the first place, France developed and sustained his literary conscience ; Mr. Bennett may have boiled the pot, but he has at least boiled it properly and not taken money for leaving it lukewarm ; never at his worst has he fallen into the disgraceful sloven-liness that spoils so much of Mr. Wells's later work ; and at his best, though he may not reach the last subtleties of construction or the ultimate felicities of style, he has shown a fine conscientious craftsmanship and has done all that a man can consciously do to bring his work near to perfection. Further, contact with French life and thought has, I imagine, sharpened his sense of the dramatic and given to his handling of any dramatic situation a certain lightness and crispness. He is not by nature a dramatist at all, because his finest work demands that background to the action which only a novelist can touch in ; and the people of his plays are not so solid as the persons in his novels mainly because he sees them as a novelist sees them ; but nevertheless he has contrived to write a number of successful and entertaining plays simply because he has good ideas, original but not too original (think of *Milestones, What the Public Wants* and *The Title*), and because he has, too, this light but sure dramatic touch. So far, this literary apostasy has brought nothing but gain ; but actually

c

there have been serious losses. Mr. Bennett, who, unlike many novelists, has always been something of a literary theorist, began writing novels at a time when he was a fervent admirer of Mr. George Moore, Maupassant and the French naturalistic school. He was a great advocate of " technique," which really meant nothing more than a suppression of the narrator and a deliberate simplicity and unity in the narrative, the action, the background. Later, in *The Author's Craft*, which is easily the best of the short talks and is really a very sensible and lucid discussion of some very difficult subjects, he admitted that his earlier attitude towards the novel was mistaken :

> With the single exception of Turgenev, the great novelists of the world, according to my own standards, have either ignored technique or have failed to understand it. What an error to suppose that the finest foreign novels show a better sense of form than the finest English novels !

What an error, indeed. The fact is, of course, that the art of fiction as practised by the great novelists *is* technique, and any other " technique " is either some inferior method or a mere catch-phrase of the pontifical critic. But Mr. Bennett began with such admirations, and in following the wrong masters did violence to his own genius. He himself is essentially a Romantic with certain ironical, sceptical twists in his mind ; and his early ideas of what a serious novel should be seem to me to have been definitely harmful, because they have made him divide his work in a fashion that has hindered his development as a great novelist. To put it shortly, the second

Mr. Bennett has never settled down to work in harmony with the third Mr. Bennett ; we have had all the rich comedy, the fantastic romance of the commonplace, the high spirits on one side, and the writer's magnificent sense of a social background, his wide sweep, his feeling for obscure and only half-articulate tragedy, his grave pity, on the other side. *The Card* is a fine tale and *Clayhanger* is a finer, but we might have had, and might still have, a story that was both the Card and Clayhanger and therefore something more, which would have been unquestionably one of the greatest works of our time. The naturalistic and realistic elements in his work have always been sadly over-emphasized by critics. He is essentially one of our English Romantics, whose feeling for romance is so strong that he can find it where most persons would never even dream of looking for it ; indeed, this may be said to be his great contribution to the English Novel. Practically all his more serious novels are simply romantic obstacle races, almost romantic conjuring tricks ; for he carefully puts away all the usual romantic trappings, shows us the most commonplace people in the dingiest and dreariest setting, takes off his coat and rolls up his sleeves, and proceeds to evolve romance. One of his first serious novels, *Leonora*, shows us that it is possible for a woman verging on middle age, the mother of grown-up daughters, suddenly to become the victim of a consuming romantic passion. Mr. Bennett himself, I imagine, must be surprised when he learns that he is regarded, as he so often is regarded, as one of the enemies of romance, only anxious to destroy the illusion by holding out for his readers' inspection the wigs and grease-paint and pasteboard castles of this life, a writer who stands chuckling with Time himself over the crumbling ruin of so many little lives. It is true, as we have seen, that he is aware, and by no means blithely aware, of the ironies of existence in such a world, and that behind his superficial convictions, his downright opinions on art and Bollinger 1911 and barbers, there lurks a mournful scepticism, but actually this only makes him more passionately attached to the romance, the dumb poetry, the hidden agonies and exultations of commonplace persons. He has made full use of the simple fact that however dull and prosaic a man may appear to others, however tedious his life may seem, to himself his life is always exciting, amazing, and he himself a daily miracle; and in three out of every four of Mr. Bennett's stories it will be found that the most piquant effects have been obtained simply by a continual contrast of what we might call the " the outside" and the "inside" views of a person's motives, actions, character. If, as I imagine, his readers so often mistake his intentions, no doubt the fault is largely his and is the result of some flaw in his art; but it is easy to see what has happened, for while the reader (of the more important novels) has naturally seen the story progressing in a forward direction, as it travels from the first chapter to the last, Mr. Bennett himself has seen the story backward, as it were, has first conceived the final situation and then worked out the rest of the tale in the light of that. The difference is important. Thus, in *The Old Wives' Tale* the reader sees the history of one of Time's innumerable conquests, the decline and fall of feminine grace and beauty, the eternal cruel process by which two exquisite girls, things of wonder, are slowly transformed into two helpless old women; but the author, while he sees all this too, really begins with a vision of two lonely old women, harmless creatures in a provincial town who would excite no comment beyond perhaps a pitying remark, and then realizes that behind them, even them, there is an epic, the play of gigantic instincts, a series of strange tragicomedies that have been secretly enacted in commonplace shops, houses, and hotels. We see the two old women and nothing more; but he sees the whole story, typical and yet marvellous, and that is his triumph. That he conceived the story in *The Old Wives' Tale* backwards is made plain in his preface to the later edition, and there can be little doubt that the same thing happened with the later tales. In the Clayhanger trilogy he probably began with a mental picture of a seemingly commonplace married couple, middle-aged, middle-class, prosperous, contented, apparently prosaic. But behind them he saw, reeling back into the 'Sixties and 'Seventies of last century, the histories of Edwin Clayhanger and Hilda Lessways, and he knew that the middle-aged ease of *These Twain* was nothing less than a port in some Fortunate Isles that the pair had only reached after incredible adventures on the high seas of youthful life. Again, he probably saw that magnificent novel, *Riceyman Steps*, from the angle of those contents-bills noted in the last chapter, "Mysterious Death of a Miser in Clerkenwell," "Midnight Tragedy in King's Cross Road," and the rest, and actually we ought to have such newspaper summaries of the story somewhere at the back of our minds when we are reading it, so that we are conscious of the piquant, or, rather, in this instance, moving contrast already noticed, the contrast here between "a sordid affair in Clerkenwell," involving one of the seediest parts of London, two misers, a simple charwoman who steals scraps of bacon, and her semi-idiotic lover, the contrast between this and the actual story as we come to know it from within, a story that has in it humanity and the world, love and death, strange loyalties and fantastic bravery, and that odd nobility and even beauty which a ruling passion, no matter how ignoble it may appear, takes on once it has secured a man's complete devotion. *Riceyman Steps*, though it lacks the epic fullness of the two great Five Towns stories and is more limited in its scope, is undoubtedly Mr. Bennett's greatest achievement as a pure craftsman, and is perhaps the best example of his disguised romantic method, of the romance that fights its way through reality when all the gates of easy appeal have been barred.

But in none of these works has the complete Mr. Bennett appeared ; something that crackles and blazes so delightfully in the lighter novels has been rigidly excluded from them, and for this exclusion, this deliberate limitation, we may perhaps thank those early views of the novel, largely formed under French influence, that have already been noticed. That influence, too, is partly responsible for a certain characteristic that is at once a virtue and a great fault in Mr. Bennett as a novelist. This is a generalizing tendency, which can be seen in everything he touches, but which is most easily observed in his treatment of love. He is, above all our other novelists, the novelist of middle-aged love ; time after time he has, for example, shown us with much humour, dramatic effect, and truth the way in which apparently bored, condescending or amused husbands, who pride themselves on a lack of sentiment, conceal in their bosoms an immense admiration, genuine passion, and solid respect for their wives ; no living novelist is better able to handle the general realities of sexual relations. But—and here he seems to me very French—the relations always remain too general ; it is always, or nearly always (for Hilda Lessways and Clayhanger perhaps provide an exception), a man and The Sex ; we are not shown the peculiar, the unique relation between two individuals, a certain man and a certain woman, but we are simply shown " an affair " in progress ; the situation is touched off very cleverly, but it is merely typical, an approximation, excellent indeed for brisk articles on married life or light comedies, but beneath the level, the highly in-dividualized level, of great fiction ; everywhere the emphasis is laid on what might be called the constant factors in sexual life, love and marriage as they appear to a psychologist and not as they should appear to an artist ; his men may be finely individualized, but they are not individualized in their sexual relations, and as for his women, they are too often simply *La Femme*, and no sooner do they make their appearance than we hear, coming faintly down the wind, the vast and endless generalizations of the Boulevards. This is not the least, but it is the last of the many limitations that must be noticed, however ungrateful it may seem, in any account of one of the most prolific, entertaining, and conscientious writers of our time. When Denry the Card was chosen as Mayor, one of his rivals, with the solemnity of a literary critic, asked what Denry had done, " what cause was he identified with," and this devil's advocate was crushed by the reply that Denry was identified " with the great cause of cheering us all up." Mr. Bennett, in his lighter work, in which he has sketched so inimitably the urban comedy of the twentieth century, is identified with the same great cause and is, indeed, a Denry of letters. In his more ambitious novels he has done something more worth while than even playing the Card, for he has taken ugly places in ugly epochs and by dint of rare understanding and noble labour has transformed their chronicles into art ; he has set a whole host of seemingly common-place persons, the people of wellnigh a whole country-side, marching down the years in that great procession which is headed by Hamlet and Falstaff, Uncle Toby and Cleopatra, Becky Sharp and Squire Western, Mr. Pickwick and the Wife of Bath.

MR. DE LA MARE

ON their last evening together on Beechwood Hill, it will be remembered, Miss M. tells Mr. Anon. of a ghost that came to a house near Cirencester : " And when it was asked, ' Are you a good spirit or a bad ? ' it made no answer, but vanished, the book said—I remember the very words—' with a curious perfume and most melodious twang.' " Mr. de la Mare himself is not unlike that ghost, for when we approach him as critics and ask him if he is this or that he, too, seems to vanish--" with a curious perfume and a most melodious twang." He is one of those writers who have a few obvious characteristics known to every-body, characteristics that are complacently indicated by the reviewer whenever such writers publish a book ; but if we wish to press forward and examine him more closely, he becomes curiously elusive, almost playing Ariel to our Caliban. There is no difficulty if we are simply prepared to enjoy and not to analyse, for we can always recognize his hand ; the work is all of a piece, and no one who has once known it can fail to appreciate that curious perfume and that most melodious twang. Superficially, his work may appear somewhat fragmentary and casual, the spasmodic creation of a gifted dilettante—a few bundles of short lyrics, some short tales, and a fantasy or two, so many lovely and quaint odds and ends ; but nothing could be further from the truth, for actually his work is one of the most individual productions this century has given us, every scrap of it being stamped with its author's personality and taking its place in the de la Mare canon. If Mr. de la Mare were to wander into half a dozen literary forms that so far have not known him, if he were to bid farewell to poetry and fiction and do nothing but essays, criticism, and even history, the new work would promptly link up with the old and take on a quality different from that of any other essays, criticism, or history, so marked is his individuality. Nevertheless, he remains to criticism an elusive figure, whose outline and gestures are not easily fixed in the memory —a shadowy Pied Piper.

One fairly common misconception must be brushed aside before we can begin to examine Mr. de la Mare, and that is the notion that he is primarily a creator of pretty fancies for the children. Because he has occasionally produced a volume for children, many persons regard him merely as the latest and most delicate of nursery poets, an artist for the Christmas Tree. Nor is this notion, except in its crudest form, confined to the uncritical, for even at this late hour there is a tendency on the part of many critics to treat Mr. de la Mare as if he were not an artist with a unique vision, a man of strange delights and sorrows, but a rather gentlemanly conjurer they had engaged for their children's party. There is, of course, an element of truth in this view, but at the moment it is hardly worth while disengaging it, though, as we shall presently see, this element of truth happens to be of supreme importance. Regarded as a general view this popular misconception is so preposterous that if we go to the other extreme, if we argue that Mr. de la Mare is a writer that no child should be suffered to approach, we shall not be further from the truth. We could point out that his work is really unbalanced, decadent, unhealthy, poisonous fruit for any child's eating. Consider his subjects. *The Return* is the story of a man who is partly possessed by an evil restless ghost, who comes back from a meditation among the tombstones in the local churchyard, wearing the face of a long-dead adventurer—a nightmare. The poetry is filled with madness and despair, wonders, and witchcraft, lit with a sinister moonlight; some crazed Elizabethan fool sitting in a charnel-house might have lilted some of these songs. The *Memoirs of a Midget* is the history of a freak who moves elvishly in the shadow of some monstrous spirit of evil; it is a long dream that never turns to the waking world, but only changes, when it does change, to nightmare. The tales in *The Riddle* are worse; they are the chronicles of crazed or evil spirits, Miss Duveen, Seaton's Aunt, and the rest; their world is one of abnormalities, strange cruelties and terrors, monstrous trees and birds and dead men on the prowl; their very sunlight is corrupt, maggot-breeding. And is this, we might ask, the writer of pretty fancies for the children; as well might we introduce Webster, Poe, and Baudelaire into the nursery and schoolroom. Such an account of Mr. de la Mare as an unwholesome decadent is manifestly absurd, but on the whole it is probably less absurd than the more popular opinion of him as a pretty-pretty children's poet. Yet we can use his work for children as a kind of jumping-off place in our pursuit of him.

We can begin with the large and very successful anthology of poetry that Mr. de la Mare has brought out recently, *Come Hither*, " a collection of rhymes and poems for the young of all ages." This very personal and delightful anthology has a curious introduction, in which very characteristically the author, by the use of quaint anagrams, makes a kind of story out of his account of Nature and Poetry ; and it also contains an enormous number of rambling notes and quotations from all manner of curious old books. And this happy volume makes it clear that when he set out to please the " young of all ages," he also set to please himself and brought together all the poetry he loved, whether it was something by Shakespeare or Milton, or an old jingle of nursery rhyme. There is about this anthology, though it contains some of the most solemn and moving passages in our literature, something of the golden spacious air of childhood, something a thousand leagues removed from the atmosphere of most anthologies of this kind, and one realizes that this is not merely the result of good taste, a sense of what is fitting, and so on, but of something much rarer, an imagina-

tion of an unusual kind, one that is infinitely wider
and more sensitive than a child's, and yet, in one
sense, still is a child's imagination. It has been said
that a keen remembrance of childhood, the ability
of a man to see again at will the world as he saw it
when a child, is a test and sign of genius. But
imagination, it is clear, includes the ability to recapture
former states of mind, whether they belong to childhood, youth or later life, and the childhood theory
of genius is obviously much too wide. It is probably
true to say that geniuses of the first rank, the Homers
and Shakespeares and Dantes, feed imaginatively on
all their experience and are no more dependent on
childhood than they are on any other period of their
life ; they are for ever gorging on existence, and as
they age, their vision widens, or at least changes.
But there is a lesser order of geniuses who create
worlds for themselves that have a distinct life of their
own, but are obviously different, running obliquely,
from the actual world we know, and it appears to
me that such writers (Dickens is the type) build up
their little universes from their childish impressions
and carry forward with them into manhood their
early imaginings and memories. What they do not
understand and cannot enter into imaginatively
during their youth they never do understand, not,
at least, for the purposes of their art. The world of
the imaginative child is made up of impressions that
are largely at the mercy of his reading. Thus the
boy who has poured over the *Arabian Nights* soon
discovers when he walks abroad that his London is

beginning to look like Bagdad, and if this impression is sufficiently strong the years may drive it away from the surface of his mind, but they will never completely destroy it ; and if our boy becomes a man of letters, then the caliph, the barber, and his brothers, and all the rest will probably find a way, beneath some disguise, into all his chapters. Dickens spent his childhood among the odd figures that loafed about Portsmouth, Chatham, and Camden Town, and his earliest reading, particularly his rapt study of Smollett, gave him a pair of spectacles through which these odd figures looked even more grotesque than they actually were, so that for the remainder of his life he moved in a world of queer shapes and violent ever-recurring gestures. Afterwards he met many new types of men and women, counting some of them among his intimates, that he tried very earnestly to portray, but he never succeeded in dowering them with that superhuman vitality which animates his other characters, for the simple reason that such persons, belonging as they did to a world he only knew later in life, never entered into his childish memories and imagination, which represented the animating principle, the pulsating heart, of all his work. A Shakespeare could have swept them all in, a Dickens could not. One mark of all the writers who belong to this class is their weakness in portraying normal, somewhat commonplace and sensible persons, who hardly exist in a child's world. Figures of terror and figures of fun, fearful or adorable monsters like Fagin and Micawber or Quilp and Mrs.

Gamp, the vast shadows thrown by a few odd personages in the flickering taper-light of a child's terror
or glee, these alone are the characters to which they
can give an intense life of their own.

It is only when they are compared with the very
greatest, the demi-gods of creative literature, that
such writers are found to be faulty, for the very
intensity of their imagining lifts them high above
the great mass of authors. Their work has a personal
vision and a curiously fascinating " glamourie " that
delights the more imaginative reader. Nor must
they themselves be supposed to be " childish " (in
the looser sense of the term) merely because the
world of their imagination was put together during
childhood, for they may have, and often do have,
the deepest feelings to express, the most subtle
emotions to convey, and their work may be quickened
with the touch of a sublime philosophy. The world
they show us may not enlarge its limitations, may
present the same colours, surfaces and shapes, but as
time goes on and their vision widens, this world
becomes more and more symbolical, just as in the
childhood of a race men people the earth and the
heavens with images of beauty and dread, the gods,
demi-gods, demons, and fairies, and these figures
persist and retain their ancient lineaments while the
race that imagined them ages and changes, making
ever-increasing demands upon the spirit, until such
figures symbolize a whole universe of complicated
values : the tale, in its outline, remains the same,
but interpretation succeeds interpretation and its

significance ever deepens. Now Mr. de la Mare, in his finest and most characteristic work, shows himself to be a writer who belongs to this order. The world he prefers to move in is one that has been pieced together by the imagination of childhood, made up of his childish memories of life and books, nursery rhymes, fairy tales, ballads, and quaint memorable passages from strange old volumes. Behind this, using it as so many symbols, is a subtle personality, a spirit capable of unusual exaltation and despair. There is nothing conscious and deliberate, I fancy, in all this ; his mind instinctively seeks these forms in which to express itself ; his imagination, when it is fully creative, instinctively avoids the world of common experience and runs back to this other world it created long ago. As a poet, he has often been compared and contrasted with Mr. W. B. Yeats, and the comparison is of special interest in this connection. Now Mr. Yeats' poetic history may be discovered in one little verse of his :

> I made my song a coat
> Covered with embroideries
> Out of old mythologies
> From heel to throat ;
> But the fools caught it,
> Wore it in the world's eyes
> As though they'd wrought it.
> Song let them take it,
> For there's more enterprise
> In walking naked.

There is a pretty little chapter of literary history in these few arrogant lines. Mr. Yeats' earlier poetry used the picturesque figures and symbolic imagery of the Celtic myths and certain mystical or pseudo-mystical cults because it found them convenient ; it wore them as a man wears a coat, and could, and did, step out of them and walk " naked " when a whole school of poets began to be attracted towards such easy and picturesque matter. Having deliberately adopted the Celtic gods and fairies, the secret roses, and what not, Mr. Yeats, who is actually nothing if not deliberate, could with equal deliberation discard such things and, further, give his reasons for doing so in verse. There is nothing instinctive here ; Mr. Yeats decided that it was high time his poetry expressed his moods under the guise of a shadowy drama of gods and fairies, and when he had had enough of it he stopped ; he has always been a very sophisticated, self-conscious artist, and appears to have always held the opinion that it was part of a poet's business to take up attitudes and play for an hour or so with the nearest mythology or the most picturesque cult. He has always been a poet who has merely dabbled in mysticism, just as his compatriot " AE " has always been a mystic who has dabbled in poetry. Whatever there is in Mr. Yeats, there is certainly as little of the child as there could be in a man who is a genuine artist, and the world of his imagination owes little to the impressions and dreams of his childhood. Now the world we discover in Mr. de la Mare's poetry has some superficial resemblance to that in Mr. Yeats', but Mr. de la Mare could not casually wave away his fairies and witches

D

and ghosts and Arabias and Melmillos and Princess Seraphitas, not because they are really anything more than exquisite images and symbols, but because they are part of a world to which his imagination instinctively turns, in which it probably actually lives, not so much a beautifully embroidered coat that his Muse wears for a season, but her actual form and presence. (Perhaps I need hardly point out that this comparison does not involve any judgment as to which is the better poet, a question that demands an altogether different approach.) One of the most beautiful and significant of Mr. de la Mare's earlier poems, *Keep Innocency*, puts before us the paradox of innocent childhood's love of what seems to its elders terrible and cruel, such as warfare :

> He, with a mild and serious eye
> Along the azure of the years,
> Sees the sweet pomp sweep hurtling by ;
> But he sees not death's blood and tears,
> Sees not the plunging of the spears.

> And all the strident horror of
> Horse and rider, in red defeat,
> Is only music fine enough
> To lull him into slumber sweet
> In fields where ewe and lambkin bleat.

> O, if with such simplicity
> Himself take arms and suffer war ;
> With beams his targe shall gilded be,
> Though in the thickening gloom be far
> The steadfast light of any star !

Though hoarse War's eagle on him perch,
Quickened with guilty lightnings—there
It shall in vain for terror search,
Where a child's eyes beneath bloody hair
Gaze purely through the dingy air.

And we may say that there is a central core in Mr. de la Mare's imagination that has " kept innocency," though his spirit should walk the awful borderlands and proclaim its despair ; a man has *felt* the world he shows us, but a child's eyes have *seen* it, lit with strange stars or bright with unknown birds.

I know nothing of Mr. de la Mare's personal history, and even if I did know something it would be sheer impertinence to make use of such knowledge here (this business is impudent enough as it is), and actually such writers whose imagination still feeds on the experience and impressions of their childhood (and by childhood I mean throughout the period up to and including adolescence) might easily have little or no common ground in their personal histories. But in order to see roughly " how it works " we can allow ourselves to indulge in a little of that not unpleasant guesswork which our newest psychologists, who are, we understand, men of science, indulge in so frequently. Here is a man, not Mr. de la Mare or another, but simply a man, who developed very early and lived more intensely than most men during his childhood, lived, let us say, in the country, and what with the sights and sounds of the country-side, old books, old houses, and quaint old people, had his fill of beauty and romance. Every object in this world would be linked with half a hundred feelings and would remain bright and clear in his memory. Everything would be significant and would not only be associated with beauty and joy, but in some instances, this being the penalty of the sensitive spirit, with terror and despair. And this boy is not only observing very closely the real world about him, discovering so many things linked up with his emotions that his very remembrance of them is infinitely suggestive, standing him in good stead in after years, but is also brooding over romance and wonders wherever he finds them, in scraps of song or tales at the fireside, and the objects and figures of romance and wonder, though they are not " real " objects and figures, take their place in his world, too, and go through the very same process that the others did, except that, as time passes, their beauty and elusiveness gives them a greater potency as symbols. His life, then, is filled, brimming over, miraculous. Then comes some disastrous change, a move from the country into some great ugly city, the death of beloved persons, the necessity of earning a living by some dull grinding occupation, and so on and so forth, and now though his life may flow evenly enough, he is already an exile, Adam has been cast forth. He begins to write, and then, like Dickens, he may release the whole flood of childish memories and impression, or like, let us say, Hawthorne, he may make little progress at first, may begin by trying to write like the persons he happens to admire at the moment and not find himself. The young man of our psychological anecdote follows the latter course, and for a time, though he produces work of exceptional interest, does not find himself; but then, as time goes on, by some chance or other, the company of children of his own, some work undertaken for children, he gradually gropes back to this central flame in his imagination and restores, or rather rediscovers for the purposes of his art, the world he has carried over from his childhood. His poetry not only makes use of the figures and situations so familiar in that world, burdening them more and more with spirit, deepening their significance, but makes more and more use of the idea of exile itself, seeing all beauty as the flaming sign that the Paradise from which we are all exiled still stands, remote but not entirely unglimpsed, and pitying all men because they are not where in their hearts they would be. His prose fables turn back more and more to that bright, clear, significant past, still burning undimmed in the memory; almost unthinkingly the very houses and furniture it describes are houses and furniture out of that boyhood; the old quaint figures come bobbing up again, the creatures of childish terror and wonder come creeping out of their holes; and every tree and bird and figure will not only be as significant as they once were, but will actually become more significant. And the work of such a man will have an unusual strength and a curious magic of its own. It will also have its own peculiar weaknesses. It will not describe with success, despite its author's knowledge of his craft, those things that only enter into adult life and the imagination of a mature man;

it will fail, as I have already suggested, with the so-called normal, in which there is no easily recognizable element of the strange, the beautiful, the terrible, the grotesque ; and in the poetry, this work will have strange weaknesses, at first unaccountable, because, though it is so concrete, like all good poetry, and dramatizes so exquisitely the fluctuations of the spirit, it will break down and lose itself in woolly abstractions when trying to express certain partly philosophical ideas, simply because such ideas are outside the range of that imaginative world ; have not, so to speak, been accepted by it, and cannot be adequately symbolized and made concrete through its agency.

So much for the theory and its pretty guesswork. A short examination of Mr. de la Mare's work, without regard for all manner of literary qualities and questions that lie outside the scope of the enquiry, will enable us to discover how closely we can apply the theory and what it is worth. But first it is worth remarking that the later work is better and more personal, more characteristic than the earlier, both in poetry and prose. Thus, both the *Memoirs of a Midget* and the collection of short tales called *The Riddle* are better, on any count, than—to go no further back—*The Return*. This last is, of course, a fantasy, but it differs from the later work not so much in its theme but in its treatment, which brings it nearer to the ordinary realistic fiction of the time than the later stories are. The style is not so mannered, not so subtly cadenced and bright with imagery, as the style of the other two volumes, and it does not lure us on to forget this world of offices and the witness-box as the later one does, but really has the contrary aim of making the one fantastic stroke credible. Mr. de la Mare has not boldly entered his own world, and the result, for all the art he has plainly lavished on the story, is unfortunate ; the story itself is one, or at least is of the kind, that we are more accustomed to seeing treated comically, in the manner, say, of Mr. Anstey, than treated tragically as it is here, and though this would not have mattered in the least had the author lured us away into his own world, it matters a great deal when he is making terms with this one. For example, seeing that the translated Lawford and his wife are compelled to deceive every one about them in the most elaborate fashion, we wonder why it did not occur to them that Lawford, who was his own master and not without means, could easily settle the matter by quietly slipping away from the district for a time. This procedure would not have pleased Mr. de la Mare, it is clear, but it was the obvious thing to do. And the author, by his method of treatment, aiming at some kind of verisimilitude, invites such questions, which would be mere prosaic quibbling, nothing more than evidence of the questioner's lack of imagination, if they were raised in connection with one of the later stories. Then again, Mrs. Lawford, a commonplace, conventionally minded wife, is the kind of character the ordinary realistic novelist sketches in between a few puffs of his (or her) cigarette ; but just where such inferior chroniclers are happily in their depth, Mr. de la Mare is well out of his, and Mrs. Lawford is appalling, a crude monster from a first novel by a third-rate writer. Her friend and their conversations are on the same level of crudity. In short, the conventional element, which would not be present at all in the later stories since the whole pack of characters, with their houses and furniture, would be subtly translated, is so badly done that it almost wrecks the fantasy, which is presented with some characteristic strokes of genius. Here, then, the normal, with its common-place tangle of adult relations and interests, has baffled our author's imagination.

Then in his next story he boldly obliterated all the common relations and affairs of life by choosing a theme that was bristling with difficulties, that probably every other story-teller we have would have rejected at a glance, but that required just such an imagination as his and no other for its successful treatment. The *Memoirs of a Midget* overshadows *The Return* not so much because it is later and the author has improved his craft, but because he has now boldly entered his own world and has left off trying to come to terms with that of most novelists. Many people have wondered why Mr. de la Mare should chose such a queer subject, the history, in autobiographical form, of a year or so in the life of a freak, for what is easily his most ambitious single performance, a novel on the old heroic scale. But if our account of him has any truth in it at all, he could hardly have done better ; the choice of subject

itself, let alone his treatment of it, was a stroke of
genius. What more effective dramatization of the
mind of an adult who still retains the imagination of
his childhood could there be than the person of Miss
M. the Midget, who is so diminutive that even the
child, to whom daisies and buttercups are platters
and chalices, is a hulking clodhopper when compared
with her, who sees an ordinary garden as a kind of
enchanted jungle :

My eyes dazzled in colours. The smallest of the marvels
of flowers and flies and beetles and pebbles, and the radiance
that washed over them, would fill me with a mute, pent-up
rapture almost unendurable. Butterflies would settle quietly
on the hot stones beside as if to match their raiment against
mine. If I proffered my hand, with quivering wings and
horns, they would uncoil their delicate tongues and quaff
from it drops of dew or water. A solemn grasshopper would
occasionally straddle across my palm, and with patience I made
quite an old friend of a harvest mouse. They weigh only
two to the half-penny. This sharp-nosed furry morsel would
creep swiftly along to share my crumbs and snuggle itself to
sleep in my lap. . . .

And yet, despite her wonder and innocence, moving
as she does in a world that is like the child's, only much
stronger and brighter, she is not a child, but a poetical
sensitive adult, with all the thoughts and emotions
of an adult who is shut off from most common
activities. And now, because it is she who tells the
story, things that would have been blemishes in
another and different story, nearer to common life,
are here in their right place ; the grotesque towering
figures, whether of Dickensian humour or of late
Byronic sentiment and tragedy, are at home in this

world, which has a reality of its own even if it is not the one we know best, and so is entitled to its own humour, sentiment, and tragedy. The style is now heightened, being very artfully cadenced and bright with pictures, particularly in the earlier, more descriptive and less dramatic chapters, which constitute, in my opinion, the best part of the book and contain the most exquisite and memorable passages, notably the description of Miss M. in the deserted house on her last evening there. All the chapters that relate to her experience at home and her early days at Mrs. Bowater's, in which she is shut off from the great world, but lives in a bright little world of her own, are magnificently done, the work of a genius ; but as her circle of acquaintance widens and she moves about more, until she queens it in London, the poetical gradually gives place to the grotesque ; the child is there and is ruthlessly inventing ; so that at times across those scenes of fashionable life, as seen by the Midget, there flutters the shadow of Mr. Salteena.

At first sight it may appear that our theory of Mr. de la Mare's imagination will break down when we pass from the *Midget*, which triumphantly proclaims its truth, to the collection of short stories in *The Riddle*. In these tales the author creeps along the borderlands of the human spirit, and in a style that is even more artful, mannered and highly coloured than that of the *Midget*, he describes the corroding evils and moonstruck fantasies that visit those on whom the world's common burden of

affairs presses most lightly, the very young and the
very old, and those whose reason has been fretted
away and whose ordinary faculties have fallen into
desuetude ;   it   is   a   book   of   " atmospheres,"   of
adventures on the edge of things, crumbling away
the homely and comforting reality, and confronting
us with the heaving and crawling darkness.   But not
all the stories are set in this queer spiritual twilight ;
some of them seem little more than exquisite memories,
clustered about some slight theme, and have something of the bright loveliness, the happy magic, of
those clear dreams that only too rarely visit our
sleep ;   their brightness and their suggestion of old
ways and scenes point to their author's having made
a poetical kind of camera obscura out of his memory.
Many   of   them   are   related   as   the   experiences   of
childhood, notably two of the most exquisite, *The
Almond Tree* and *The Bowl*, both of which have the
air of being fragments from some greater context
(though perhaps existing only in the writer's mind) ;
and none of these things could have been created
by a man who had not kept alive his childhood and
never lost sight of its world.   Some of the tales have
the appearance of bright nursery pictures that have
suffered some curious change and become symbolical
representations of a spiritual life that no nursery
ever knew.   And even the stories that seem furthest
away from anything we can connect with childhood
reveal, after some scrutiny, their indebtedness to the
kind of imagination that has already been described.
No reader of that excellent tale, *The Tree*, is ever

likely to confuse Mr. de la Mare's Fruit Merchant
with the actual elderly wholesale greengrocers who
do business in the neighbourhood of Covent Garden,
for this Fruit Merchant, with his triangular nose and
small bleak black eyes, first appears to the imagination like one of the quaint figures in a toy-book and
finally remains in it as some kind of bad fairy, who
could only traffic in apples of glass and oranges from
the Dead Sea. Only the trade directories in the
kingdom of Oberon can have known the fantastic
firm of Lispet, Lispett and Vaine. And there could
hardly be a better example of the way in which it is
possible to utilize a figure from the world of the
imaginative child, making it return with all its
suggestion of terror, but deepening its significance,
than the figure of Seaton's monstrous aunt in the
story of that name. The spiritual background of
the story can only be understood by an adult, but
the principle figure, this eccentric old woman with
her long face, big head, and enormous appetite, who
is somehow a witch and a devil, comes straight out
of childish memory and imagination, and no man
who has completely lost his childhood will feel any
terror in her presence ; in our maturity we meet
eccentric old ladies, but no such aunts as this ; but
our early days and nights, if we had any imagination
at all, were peopled with such creatures. There is
a curious suggestion throughout these stories (as I
pointed out in another place when *The Riddle* first
appeared) that this world of Mr. de la Mare's is, as
it were, the other half of the Dickens' world, the

poetical, mysterious, aristocratic half that Dickens, with his eyes fixed on the democratic, humorous, melodramatic elements, never gave us. This suggestion was something more than an odd fancy, for both these lovable geniuses (Mr. de la Mare is certainly a genius), different as they are in almost every essential, have at least one thing in common, their method of building up their worlds, the process of the creative imagination.

Fortunately Mr. de la Mare's poetry has been more frequently noticed and more widely quoted than his prose, so that we need only touch upon its essentials. Its world, as we have seen, is one that has largely been made up of the impressions of childhood. Nursery rhyme, ballad, fairy tale, quaint memories have run together and formed a world that is filled with curious symbolism, romantic images, and a haunting elusive music that is like nothing so much as the exquisite stammer of some elfin-hearted girl. And nothing less than music and strange imagery that hangs upon one miraculous adjective could express what the poet has in his heart. We have seen already that such a poet would make more and more use of the idea of exile itself, and an examination of the poetry only confirms the opinion. In his very acute short study, Mr. Shanks remarked :

He is, in the first place, the poet of lost paradises. Almost all his poetry expresses dissatisfaction with this world, with this life, and a straining towards something more to be desired, which is indescribable, almost unimaginable, of which an image is evoked as it were between the words of his poems.

If he has one constant and recurring thought about the world it is this—that there is a better place to be in than the one in which we now find ourselves. . . .

This is very true. It is, after all, but a step from the exile from childhood to the exile from Paradise. Mr. de la Mare's delight in the world (and some of his loveliest poems are expressions of that delight, and what is perhaps his very finest poem, *Farewell*, is noble praise of it) only leads him away from life, that is, not the whole cosmic process, but the battle between belly and worm that stirs the surface of this planet ; and every lovely thing only increases his desire to glimpse :

> Pure daybreak lighten again on Eden's tree.

and when he wishes to praise music, as so many poets have done, it is characteristic of his most constant mood that he should praise it because it remakes the world or lifts the shades of the prison-house for an hour :

> When music sounds, gone is the earth I know,
> And all her lovely things even lovelier grow. . . .

He will put his songs into the mouths of those who are " simple happy mad," because such Fools, carolling on the blasted heaths of life, are still as children, have kept innocency. In the volume called *Motley*, the influence of the war is apparent everywhere, and yet it takes a form different from that in the work of other poets. Characteristically Mr. de la Mare prefers to treat it as a child might treat some inexplicable calamity, like the sudden death of a parent ;

his momentary despair takes on the character of a child's outraged innocence, and a catastrophe that was brought about by the human will can only force its way into his world in the guise of some insane and hardly credible intrusion, as if a mad bull had rushed into Miss M.'s garden. Not that he is wanting in ordinary human sympathy, coldly detached; on the contrary, as some critics have already pointed out, pity, a boundless noble charity, is probably the dominant note of his work. Whatever it is that he has lost and now regrets, whether it is childhood, platonic pre-existence, eternity, Paradise, that the flash of a bird's wing or the glimpse of a burning face recalls for a moment, it is not merely for the saved or the sensitive; if he is an exile, then so are all men, and so his pity is universal. And his greatest weakness, as I suggested in an earlier passage, is his failure to express certain ideas in the concrete imagery that poetry demands, his tendency to find refuge in vague and woolly abstractions; and this weakness is easily understood when we realize that a poetic imagination like his is clearly limited and is unable to grapple with ideas that belong entirely to maturity. If there ever was a body of lyrical verse that embodied, with exquisite precision, a definite philosophical attitude towards life, it is the poetry of Mr. A. E. Housman, yet no contemporary verse is more concrete, less given to abstractions. But Mr. Housman's imaginative world is not the product of childhood (and so lacks the romantic glamour, the fascinating strangeness of Mr. de la Mare's) but of early manhood, and is thus able to provide the appropriate dramatic and concrete setting (or body) for his ideas. But this weakness is less marked in Mr. de la Mare's last volume, *The Veil*, which is stronger and harsher, not without traces of growing pains on the part of its author, so that it may well be that he will make this theory of his genius, sketched in so crudely, out of date before it has been more carefully stated and developed. In the meantime he remains one of that most lovable order of artists who never lose sight of their childhood, but re-live it continually in their work and contrive to find expression for their maturity in its memories and impressions, its romantic vision of the world; the artists whose limitations and weaknesses are plain for any passing fool to see, but whose genius, and they are never without it, never mere men of talent, delights both philosophers and children; the artists who remember Eden.

MAURICE HEWLETT'S
LATER VERSE AND PROSE

MAURICE HEWLETT was his own best example. He would have us all return to poverty and plain living, and there find ourselves ; and he himself did return, as it were, to verbal poverty and plain speaking, planted his feet firmly upon the earth, and indeed found himself. There could be no better illustration of the successful working of his theory, and it is a great pity that he was debarred from using it. This change in Hewlett's matter and manner has already been noticed, but it has not had the attention it deserves. In the Preface to his *Wiltshire Essays*, our author himself has complained bitterly of the way in which he is still confused in the public mind with the frolics of his youth :

Notwithstanding that full five-and-twenty years have coursed over this frosted pow since I belauded the youth of Italy, notwithstanding that I have published seven volumes of poems, and scarcely a volume in prose which was not conceived as a poem is conceived, it is still the fact that six readers out of ten expect every new book of mine that reaches them to be more or less an echo of *The Forest Lovers*. What am I to do ? It imputes to me incredible stupidity, itself is incredibly stupid—and what can one do with stupidity except foam at the mouth ? Somebody sent me a specimen of his prowess

in that kind only the other day, a chuckle-headed " K.K."
writing in I know not what journal. "Admirers of Mr.
Hewlett's graceful pen," he said—or words to that effect—
" will be disappointed when they open *In a Green Shade* and
find that it is not a swashbuckling romance . . ." And so on.
What are you to do ?

There was, of course, nothing to be done, except to
peg away and to keep one's temper. An artist with
a love of experiment in this country is in a mournful
situation : if he is unsuccessful, it does not matter
what he does, because nobody cares ; but if he
suddenly becomes successful, he then develops into
a kind of institution and people go to him for little
pictures of two cows in a field, or paradoxical essays,
or swashbuckling romances, and are as surprized and
resentful if they find anything else there as they
would be if they went to a billiard saloon and discovered a lecture on relativity in progress.

Before the publication of *The Song of the Plow*, an
event that we may regard as the turning point,
Hewlett had proved himself, at least to all who used
their eyes and did not blindly follow literary fashions,
to be one of our cleverest, most versatile and delightful men-of-letters. Somewhat tentatively I make
this reservation about those who followed fashions,
because I have a fancy that he was probably a little
underestimated by the bright advance-guards of
criticism, if only because he elected to follow romance
at a time (after the Stevensonian wave had expended
itself) when romance was going out of fashion and
the realistic and sociological manners were becoming

the vogue. Verse, very mannered, on classical and mediæval themes; some rather wooden Icelandic adventures; mediæval and Italian tales, all colour and bloom and fine airs; one closely knit historical romance, *The Queen's Quair*; some stories, very artfully contrived, of the Regency period; and a trilogy of modern novels, which contained some particularly irritating personages; these were the wares he brought to market in those days, bright glittering stuff that could never cumber any stall for long. At the risk of appearing ungrateful, however, it must be admitted that there was about all these things just that suspicion of the masquerade, that delight in adopting and maintaining a difficult attitude, that fully conscious zest in verbal jugglery and literary play in general, which mark the man whose talent and energy are vastly superior to his themes, the author whose powers of expression are better than his powers of conception, the brilliant crotchety amateur, or perhaps the professional at the playful, decorative stage, the Shakespeare of *Love's Labour's Lost*. Hewlett did some magnificent work, and always showed himself an artist, bent on grappling with and overcoming new difficulties, and not a manufacturer, turning out the required article; but nevertheless I do not think he ever completely found himself; his work had echoes of other voices in it, and often suggested that its author had derived his inspiration at second-hand, from other books, rather than from his own interpretation of what was stirring about him; and always it looked as if the

man was greater than his theme and task, and so
was able to show off his jugglery and sleight-of-hand.
He might have been called *The Stooping Author*.

The change comes with *The Song of the Plow*, that
epic of the labouring countryman which was an old
project of his and perhaps one that he was so doubtful
of ever realizing that, very generously, he presented
it to one of his creatures, Gervase Poore, the poet
who rhapsodizes and glooms through *Mrs. Lancelot*
and *Bendish*. The poem itself, however, is only
one, though, I think, the finest, manifestation of
Hewlett's faith, and it is to this faith that we must
turn. His general attitude, which must be described,
but need not, I think, be criticized in this place, is
easily discovered, for, leaving the poems on one side,
in all his three books of essays he sturdily pronounces
his creed and is nothing if not dogmatic. It is
essentially the attitude of a poet of an aristocratic
temper who, returning to the country, has found in
the people there, or at least in those of them whom
he chooses to call the Peasantry, that stability and
respect for tradition which seem to make a welcome
and kindly retreat from the Walpurgis night of
modern ideas. He takes his stand upon tradition, is
a determined anti-intellectual, and appears to entertain a hearty contempt for our recent panaceas. In
his first preface, he remarks :

The point is that, having worked hard for a good many
years, I can now consider my latter end under conditions
favourable to leisurely and extended thought, sometimes in
a garden made, if rightly made, in my own image, sometimes

in a house which was built aforetime, in a day when men wrought for posterity as well as for themselves. In such seed-plots it is impossible that one's thoughts should not take colour as they rise. Whithersoever I look I see as much permanency as is good for any sojourner upon earth ; I see embodied tradition, respect for Nature's laws, attention to beauty, subservience to use ; all this within doors. Outside, the trees, the flowers are my calendar ; the birds chime the hours ; periodically the church-bell calls the travellers home.

And a little further on he comes to closer grips with his matter :

I have my pet nostrums, of course. I believe in Poverty, Love and England, and am convinced that only through the first will the other two thrive. I want men to be gentlemen and women to be modest. I want men to have work and women to have children. . . .

The essays that follow, in all three books, hardly ever lose sight of these axioms. Dean Inge could not make Hewlett's flesh creep, because the picture the Dean paints of our last and worst state, when we are once more " a small, hardy, fishing, and pastoral people," is the very picture that delighted Hewlett, who boldly declared :

Personally, I not only believe that, but (and there perhaps I part company with the Dean) look forward to it. My one regret is that I shall not be alive to see it. A confederation of the size of ours will be a more unconscionable time a-dying than King Charles was. I remember once writing that if a little England was good enough for Queen Elizabeth and Sir Walter Raleigh, it was good enough for me ; but what is perhaps more to the purpose is to point out that, before the war, and I think also since, the smallest nations of Europe have held the highest proportion of happy and prosperous citizens : Belgium, Holland, Denmark, Switzerland. It is difficult also to see how it can be, if poverty makes contentment for an individual, that it should not for a group of individuals, a nation. I, who was once rich and now am poor, seriously declare that I had not the gleam of a notion what contentment was until I became as I am.

But Hewlett's optimism was grounded upon his belief, which he shared with Mr. Belloc and Mr. Chesterton, in the Peasantry :

> There is one class or nation of men, which he (Dean Inge) has lost sight of altogether, and that is the Peasantry. So long as that class can be contentedly settled here, with sons to marry and daughters to be married, there is no fear of degeneration. That brings me to a most curious conclusion ; for that nation of men, which may be our last, was also our first. The Peasantry in this island has survived some two thousand years of servitude ; and though it is now relatively small, it is not so small but that it can replenish our country. . . . I daresay it can be asserted of every country in Europe, west of the Adriatic, that its peasantry was the first of men there, and will be the last to go. They are, as it were, the very stone-crop, the flowers of the field. The Dean deplores the approaching extinction of his own class. It will not be extinguished if it once more mates with the Peasantry.

In another place, discussing the possible departure of Capital from this island and with it a large proportion of our population, industrial workers and the like, he describes the situation in which the remnant will find itself :

> Of what, of whom, will the remnant consist ? Of those, firstly, so rooted in the soil of this England that they cannot be torn out of it ; our agricultural, fishing, seafaring, small-trading population, the first here, the last to go, the soundest, healthiest, steadiest, most laborious, most patient of our nation. They will be, as they have generally been, the nucleus. Others will be added to whom the call of tradition, ancestry,

association, and what we know as the heartstrings, outvails that of luxury and ease; others again who have religious, sentimental, philosophical inklings of the blessings of poverty, chastity and obedience. Many of the adventurous will remain to probe a new life which cannot fail of adventure, and of much more adventure than the old; for when you have everything there is nothing to get; and when you have nothing there is everything. Scientists, artists, men of letters (but not " best-sellers ") ; clergymen, lawyers, doctors—all of these : in fine, any class of men to which, when leisure of mind is in the balance, easy money is not the prime good. There's for the remnant.

That is as far as we need go, sociologically, though Hewlett gives us more detailed views of the matter in his *Extemporary Essays*. But everywhere, it is clear, he clings to the countryman, the Peasant, because it is he who follows tradition, worships Saint Use (as Hewlett phrases it in more than one place), whereas in every other class, our author, with something like terror, sees tradition failing. Capital snarls and Labour roars ; masters will not pay and workmen will not work ; husbands will not cherish their wives and wives will not obey their husbands ; unsavoury and lawless adventures are all too common ; young men are without faith and for ever jeer at authority ; young women smoke and loll and either have babies without husbands or husbands without babies ; there is little faith and few works ; and all classes show the same symptoms ; but the Peasantry, out of reach of fashion and abiding by the old ways, the least of all ; so let us cherish the Peasantry. This is Hewlett's doctrine, and it is worth remarking that he had been driven to accept it by two special needs that belong to the two different capacities in which he chose to act. He was, first, a poet. It is his own description of himself, and it is quite accurate :

> If I am to deal with life it must be in my own way, for there's no escape from one's character. I may be a good poet or a bad one—that's not for me to say ; but I am a poet of sorts. Now a poet does not observe like a novelist. He does not indeed necessarily observe at all until he feels the need of observation. Then he observes, and intensely. He does not analyse, he does not amass his facts ; he concentrates. He wrings out quintessences ; and when he has distilled his drops of pure spirit he brews his potion. Something of the kind happens to me now, whether verse or prose be the Muse of my devotion. A stray thought, a chance vision, moves me ; presently the flame is hissing hot. Everything then at any time observed and stored in the memory which has relation to the fact is fused and in a swimming flux. Anon, as the Children of Israel said to Moses, " There came forth this calf."

Now the advantage to a poet of such a doctrine as that which Hewlett held is that it is at once simple and emotional, and being based largely upon tradition, it is, as it were, half-poetized already. Most modern social and political doctrines are useless to the poet as a poet, although he may accept one or other of them in his private capacity as a thoughtful citizen, simply because they are much too complex and do not lend themselves to poetical treatment. Our present intellectual state-socialism, for example, with its statistics and committees of enquiry and minority reports, is clearly a prose affair. Shelley's doctrine of universal revolt and love and human perfectibility had the necessary simplicity, it was the kind of large, sweeping gesture that becomes a poet, but it was entirely cut off from tradition, and Shelley always had to leave the earth and take everything into his own rarefied upper air. Fortunately for Hewlett, who was no Shelley, his own doctrine demanded no such flights, but stood rooted in the soil and fetched colour and bloom from all his readers' memories, for however much we may be opposed to tradition, it has always an advocate in our remembered emotions, our older memories, laid away in lavender, so that a poet who takes his stand upon tradition may be said to have half won his reader before he has set down a word. But during the last ten years of his life, Hewlett was not only a poet, he was also what we may call, for want of a better word, a moralist. He had always a sharp eye for a man, a delight in character, but in his last years, he not only tried to understand, he judged; he was not content merely to explain a man, but always went on to pass sentence, not arbitrarily or harshly, on the one hand, nor with that irritating god-like detachment, on the other, but as a man who has lived his life, discovered for himself what there is of good and evil in it, and set up his standards accordingly; as a man, at once passionate and thoughtful, might speak of his neighbours. His biographical interests are easily discovered in his essays, and it is significant that he preferred to review biographies, memoirs, letters, and so on; in short, any books that showed him a fellow human being. As he was a moralist, he had to have standards to which he could refer every phase of conduct; as he was an elderly moralist, he disliked the looseness and laxity of these later times ; and as he was a poet and not a philosopher, he did not try to invent an ethical system of his own ; so that here again we may say that he was almost compelled to take his stand upon tradition, which demanded that men should work and have faith and that women should be pure and bear children. Thus, the poet and the moralist joined hands.

This brings us to his capital achievement, *The Song of the Plow*. Not only is it his capital achievement, but it is also the best long poem (it has nearly five thousand lines) of our time, and perhaps it is the most neglected. The persons who are for ever crying out for sustained work from our poets, who ask for strong meat, something to get their teeth into, in short, the critics, are the very persons who are responsible for this sad neglect. Thus, for example, at the time when the poem was first published, in the autumn of 1916, the one weekly review entirely devoted to literature and the arts, the *Athenæum*, gave the *Song of the Plow* (which appears in its index as the *Sons of the Plow*) a beggarly two hundred words or so of very faint praise, clearly dominated by the conviction of the reviewer, who evidently favoured an a priori method of criticism, that it was impossible to write an epic on the subject of Hodge. Again, in the three supplementary volumes of the *Encyclopædia Britannica* that cover the last ten years, there is an article on the literature of the period, fairly long, authoritative, and bristling with names, but nowhere in this article is there any mention of the *Song of the Plow*. This omission is serious, but the next one takes us into the realm of pure farce, for not only is the poem not given any mention in the general article, but it is also omitted from the list of works in the short article devoted to Hewlett himself; everything is mentioned but this one great work, the poet's own darling; it is as if *Paradise Lost* were to be omitted from a bibliography of Milton. Not all the critics were so blind, of course, for one or two of them strove hard to secure some recognition for the poem and did at least succeed in carrying it into its second edition, where it seems to have remained in a decent obscurity ever since. Many of us who were busy with other things in the autumn of 1916 probably glanced at the poem, noted, with approval, its robust masculine air, and quietly rejoiced in the fact that there was at least one poet who was not indulging in either patriotic rant, on the one hand, or egotistical whining, on the other; but having done this, we probably allowed both the poem and its author to fade out of our memory. To turn back to the poem now is to do more than recapture our first admiration for it; for high above the ruined contraptions of stucco, lath, and plaster it rises like a monument. A fine generous mood has been caught and fixed for ever.

As we have seen, Hewlett's beliefs made it possible for him to attempt a long poem with some chance of success, for they were grounded upon tradition and were at once simple and passionate, and therefore ripe for poetry. But a faith, however passionately it may be held, will not carry an epic to a triumphant conclusion ; that most difficult form demands faith, passion, sincerity, but it also demands exquisite craftsmanship, and it is Hewlett's craftsmanship that must engage our attention. At a first glance, the general scheme of the poem is very attractive and suggests no special difficulties. Hewlett believed that the peasantry of this country, represented by the figure of Hodge, really form a separate nation (they are British with a strong English mixture of blood, as opposed to the governing class, which is Latin-French), and it is the history of this governed race from the Norman Conquest up to our own time with which he presents us in the *Song of the Plow*. In his Preface, he puts the argument in Aristotle's manner :

> *A certain man, being in bondage to a proud Conqueror, main-*
> *tained his customs, nourisht his virtues, obeyed his tyrants, and*
> *at the end of a thousand years found himself worse off than he*
> *was in the beginning of his servitude. He then lifted his head,*
> *lookt his master in the face, and his chains fell off him.*

And one does not need to be a poet to realize the attraction of such a theme. Kings come and go, armies march and countermarch, men talk in Parliament or rot on gibbets, but through it all, Hodge remains at his plow and bears upon his broad back all the fighting and junketing, the coloured prides and gilded treacheries, of those whose very existence is to him nothing but a strange rumour, a moving splash of colour on the road, a little jangling noise in the distance. The seasons return and with them his round of cares, and these are permanent while all else shifts and fades or goes clanging down to its doom. But we are not to be treated to a bucolic idyll; we are to see:

> Hodge crucified,
> Like Him Who on His rood hung bare!

we are to hear:

> . . . . the grumbled low refrain,
> The broken heartstrings' undertones
> Which thro' the clash and gallant strain
> Of warring legions, thro' the groans
> Of them they war on, thro' the blent
> Organs and trumpets, creaks and drones
> The lordings' way to tournament,
> To love of women, pride of men,
> To crowning or to parliament.

And there are two great difficulties in front of the poet. In the first place, in order to carry out his scheme, he has to sketch for us almost a thousand years of English agrarian history, a subject with which Hewlett's work in the Land Records Office made him familiar. But rhymed history is one thing, and poetry another. There is, it is clear, a dead weight of material here that will have to be given life and movement, touched with emotion, and transformed into something shining and beautiful. Every epic poet has to face this difficulty. Instead of lifting it up, giving everything in it a touch of sublimity, as, for example, Milton did with his great argument, Hewlett, having very different matter to vivify, adopted another method; he preferred to sing rather than to chisel, and forced the whole mass into swift movement by the sheer force of his passion. It was, however, his choice of metre that enabled him to send his learning skimming down the full tide of his passionate song. Knowing and loving his Dante, he elected to write his epic in *terza rima*, but unlike most of our experimenters, for example, Shelley and R. W. Dixon (who used *terza rima* in his long poem *Mano*), Hewlett very wisely decided for a short and vigorous line, namely, the octosyllabic. Handling this unusual measure with great dexterity, he was able to be passionate, scornful and pitiful in turn, for in his hands the measure combines something of the tightness and hardness of the epigrammatic modes with the clash and ring, the swift forward movement of the ballad. Without ever sacrificing the unity that the poem demands, he can yet satisfy half a dozen different moods. He can paint a picture with a few broad strokes :

> Behold them on the sky-line thrown
> Like giant shapes of riven rock,
>   He and his team on the world's rim
>   Creeping like the hands of a clock.
> Or in wet meadows plashy and dim
>   When winter winds blow shrill and keen,
>   See him bank up the warp and swim
> The eddying water over the green ;
>   Or follow up the hill the sheep
>   To where the kestrels soar and lean,
> And from her form the hare doth leap
>   Quick and short, and lightly flies
>   Before him up the grassy steep
> Where cloakt and crookt he climbs. . . .

Or he can suddenly swoop down from his eagle's
height, and give us a flash of drama, as he does so
finely in the passage on the Black Death :

> . . . . John Stot's wife died
>   A Tuesday, when John Stot was gone
>   To work three hours. The children cried
> And pulled her gown. The eldest one
>   Scolded and husht them. " Look," said she,
>   " The pretty spot my finger's on.
> Tis like a gilly flower. And see
>   Here's another ! " Then she stared
>   And stiffened, and lookt fixedly ;
> And tho' they throng'd her knees she glared
>   Up at the rafters ; and the spot
>   Glow'd on another armpit bared.
> Then all her troubles were forgot,
>   And there was left one out of five
>   To wait, but not to see, John Stot.

Or he can sum up, in a few splendid lines, the attitude
of his people throughout an age, as, for example,
when he writes of Hodge in the great days of early
exploration :

> He pastures on the common grass
>   Week in and out ; he cannot stand
> To see the questing carvels pass
>   Before the wind, a glory of white
>   Upon the gray sea's emptiness ;
> Or watch them top the edge of light
>   And be no more than a wandering name
>   Heard in the day and lost at night.
> To him the West wind brought no fame
>   Of Greenland or still Labrador,
>   When Cabot home to Bristol came
> And the old world knew one world more ;
>   His heart beat not to hear the horn
>   Shrill from the East the open door.

And, finally, he can change his note entirely, and can dispose of innumerable historical figures and events in a few shrewd and biting lines. Here is a typical passage in this vein :

> They changed a dullard for a rogue
>   When a fourth George reign'd in his stead ;
> Who made adultery the vogue
>   At Court, and wail'd his griefs aloud
>   When his wife swell'd the catalogue
> Of them who seeded what he plow'd.
>   After him raced the rout of shame,
>   The lewd, the fond, the empty-proud—
> Alvanley, Yarmouth, Jersey's dame,
>   The Beau, the Poodle, in carouse,
>   While England sicken'd at the game ;
> And all the wit of Holland House,
>   All Bowood's talk and Woburn's treasure,
>   Spent not the value of a louse
> On goaded men's content or pleasure.

But a consideration of this last passage, and of those immediately surrounding it, brings us to a point that must be made, namely, that while Hewlett did magnificently, he did not entirely succeed in fusing all his matter into poetry and avoiding rhymed history. It was not to be expected. In the last two or three books, which cover the last hundred and fifty years, the historical matter tends to overwhelm the poet ; he handles it to our admiration ; the wit, the lightning judgments, the force and grim humour, are astonishing; but we cannot help feeling that the song has flagged and the music has been transformed into a series of blows on an anvil. Fortunately, the Envoy, that moving and generous vision of New Domesday recaptures the song, and we come to the end in a maze of swift music and bright speech, our hearts warming to the man who made it all. From the very first line—" I sing the Man, I sing the Plow "—to the very last—" God speed the plow ! The tale is told "—the poem is a magnificently sustained piece of writing, masculine in style, close in grain, yet passionate and moving, keeping a close hold upon its great theme and yet so brimmed with soft and lovely images of the country-side and the life there that the poet is often in danger of defeating his purpose by making us feel that Hodge's is the most rather than the least enviable lot ; it is the creation, the long but happy labour, of a generous thinker, a strong personality, a fine craftsman ; it is the work, downright, full-blooded, proffered without stint, of a man, and men should honour it.

In the Envoy to the *Song of the Plow* there is much that brings back to our remembrance (as we smile somewhat wryly) the generous emotions, the hopeful spirit, that we knew in the early days of the War. In Hewlett's other long poem, *The Village Wife's Lament*, which was published two years afterwards, in 1918, the change in mood is very noticeable ; it is the fourth year of the War and we have gone from the major into the minor key. The poem itself is much shorter than the *Song of the Plow*, much less ambitious, and, I think, taking into account its more limited aim, not so successful ; but nevertheless it has a curious interest and appeal of its own, and is indeed, in many respects, unique. It is partly a

F

narrative poem and partly an elegy, and gives us the story of a young country-woman, widowed in the War, who describes very simply her early life and courtship, her marriage and subsequent happiness, and finally the loss of both her husband and child ; a stark and desolate piece. Hewlett himself said that the poem was dramatic and that he could not be supposed answerable for all that it expressed ; but it is quite clear that, in writing the poem, he had two objects in view. In the first place, he wished to make it dramatic and so far satisfying as a poem ; and in the second, he also wished to make it the vehicle of a number of ideas that he held very strongly at the time and that were to find expression in other places, notably in his essays. Thus, through the agency of his village wife, he wished to show us the simple dignity of the type to which she belonged (and particularly its loyalty and purity in sexual matters, upon which he was always insistent), the purely chivalrous attitude of the English peasantry, who knew nothing of world politics, when they offered themselves as soldiers in the early days of the War, and above all the pacific and Quaker-like attitude of mind that he himself came to adopt about the time the poem was written, an attitude that is well expressed in the naïve and poignant cries of the stricken girl :

> O what is this you've done to me,
>   Or what have I done,
> That bare should be our fair roof-tree,
>   And I all alone ?

Yet all this is a great deal to expect of one poem, and it is not surprising that Hewlett did not quite succeed in accomplishing everything he set out to do ; there is some loss, and that, I think, chiefly on the dramatic side, for the village wife too often fades for a space into a symbolic figure expressing general ideas rather than personal grief and bewilderment. The loss would have been much greater had not Hewlett, with rare austerity, foresworn the richer devices of his craft and chosen the simplest form and the barest language he could find. Indeed, he staked everything upon the moving appeal, the naïveté and poignancy, of the figure he presents to us, and did not hesitate to give us such things as this :

> For we were knit, no doubt of it,
>   I as well as he ;
> I peered in glass, my eyes were lit
>   After he lookt at me.
>
> I knew not why my heart was glad,
>   Or why it leapt, but so 'tis,
> The sharpest, sweetest pang I've had
>   Was when he took notice.

The rough ballad measure in which the poem is written, with its jerkiness and awkwardness, and its heavy internal rhymes :

> Or shockhead boy, aburst with joy,
>   Or gawky, ill-at-ease,
> All hot and coy, a hobbledehoy
>   With laces round his knees—

and so on, has no charm of its own, but actually the apparent faults, the monotony, the angularity, the repetition, really give the poem its poignancy ; it is either a cry, heartfelt, terrible, or it is nothing ; and the reader who cannot find beauty in it (there are certainly few " beauties " in it) but discovers that it is distasteful to him, must be really influenced by a thorough distaste for the sight and sound of simple grief, of which this poem is perhaps the most adequate expression in our recent literature. That this stark and naked thing should have been written at all by an author who was commonly thought of as a lord of fine language and purple phrases, is, if nothing else, yet one more proof of his astonishing versatility.

Hewlett himself thought the essay a species of talk (it is a view that needs considerable modification), and certainly his own essays suggest talk, at once brilliant and sensible, familiar but pared down to the essentials. In them, the poet, the moralist, the critic, scholar and biographer, and the man of the world, all have room in which to play. He was too impatient to be a good critic, but nevertheless his essays on literary subjects are amazingly good, a kind of sketch-criticism, at once stimulating and provo-cative, and usually taking the form of a rapid but by no means superficial examination of literature from some particular angle. Thus, in an essay entitled *The Facts* in his last volume, after establishing it that in lyric poetry there is a sublimity discernible which depends for its power upon fact alone, upon plainness of statement and perfect clearness, he runs at top speed through the gardens, groves, and thickets of our poetry and points out a flower there, a tree

here, as he passes. But more frequent are the essays
in which he examines a literary figure, it may be
Bessy Moore, seen through her husband's diary, or
Shelley and Mary (*The Children Who Ran Away*) as
they are discovered in her *Life and Letters*, or Byron
as he is in his correspondence with Lady Melbourne.
Of the last-named, Hewlett remarked :

> To anyone who knows what there has been to know about
> Byron, it is obvious that he was a coxcomb ; a young man
> without judgment, or morals, or truth, or conduct, or manners.
> There are things in these letters which prove him to have been
> a cad, others which show him to have been a blackguard. . . .

which passage is an excellent example of his manner,
which is sharp, short, and decided. He had thought
about these things for years, and he had made up his
mind, and so everywhere he spoke his mind, in a curt,
clear-cut, very personal prose that has a salt flavour
and a frosty sparkle in it ; but he did it without having
that desire to astonish which is so common among
our younger men. However combative, sententious,
and sharp he might be, in his last days, he was, unlike
so many of his best-known contemporaries, an author
and not an irritant. He was, however, at times a
little too tart, too much the elderly moralist, more
anxious to condemn than to understand and apt to
forget that the world as it stands is the work of the
older and not the younger generation ; but at his
very worst he was never sour and never far from
humour, which had a habit of " breaking in " even
in his gravest homilies. Apart from these literary
papers, his essays may be said to be the prose com-

mentary upon his poetry; they handle the same themes, but in a very different manner; and as the same ideas run through them all, there is in consequence a certain amount of repetition. Hewlett contributed most of these papers to periodicals, and often they deal with more or less topical themes which he examined in the light of his own particular beliefs, so that while there is repetition, it is never exact repetition; we cover the same ground, as it were, but are not taken the same walk. Essayists are, I fear, a little given to repeating themselves, and they are also given, even the best of them, to padding; but in all Hewlett's three volumes there is, I imagine, less padding, more solid matter to the page, than there is in any one book by any contemporary essayist. By suddenly turning journalist late in life he quietly made for himself a little niche in miscellaneous prose literature that he will continue to occupy. As in his poetry, so in his later prose, he gave us his best, wrote from the heart, and made not only readers, but friends. If we did not give him sufficient praise when he was alive, neglected him shamefully when he was doing his finest work, we can at least make amends now, and add to our own felicity, by taking his later books to our hearts. He would not have asked for anything better.

THE POETRY OF MR. A. E. HOUSMAN

MR. A. E. HOUSMAN is easily our most surprising poet. His first surprise was *A Shropshire Lad* itself, one of the most astonishing volumes in a very astonishing literature. It came to us practically a full-grown masterpiece, and the production of what used to be regarded as a lyric poet's maturity. He gave us no interesting juvenilia to examine; we have never seen the beginnings, when he was working under half a dozen conflicting influences, when his own manner was only half developed. His next surprise was to maintain an almost unbroken silence for over a quarter of a century—to be exact, from 1896 to 1922. As time went on it seemed to us that he had said what he had had to say in a clear, unfaltering voice, and then, having eased his heart, had passed on in silence. It was as if a man in a noisy crowded company had suddenly broken his silence with a few golden words, and had then closed his lips for ever. But no, in the autumn of 1922 there came, out of the blue, his third surprise, a new volume of lyrics bearing the characteristic title—*Last Poems*. About a quarter of it was written that year, but the remainder of the poems belong to a period between 1895 and 1910. It is not what most people, who do not know

77

their man, would expect it to be ; it is not a scrapbook, nor does it show us the spectacle of a writer trying to parody himself ; it is as little senile as the earlier volume was juvenile ; it is the *Shropshire Lad* over again, neither better nor worse, but naturally some-what different, a little lacking in the lyrical freshness of the earlier poems, but often freer and bolder, and here and there (particularly in the nightmarish *Hell Gate*) breaking new ground. There is no reason why these two volumes, with the poems kept in their present order, should not be bound up together to form the two sections of one complete volume, which should be given the covering title of *A Shrop-shire Lad*. This last point can hardly be disputed, and it seems to me important, mainly because Mr. Housman has carried over the peculiar method of the earlier book (which, as we shall see, may be called " dramatization ") into the later one, which therefore cannot be fully appreciated unless it is understood to be the *Last Poems of A Shropshire Lad*. For this reason I need make no apology for treating these two volumes, only containing one hundred odd short lyrics in all, as one, and for occasionally referring to them collectively as *A Shropshire Lad*.

In a certain volume that professes to review the poetry of the last thirty years, a volume that deals at some length with all manner of poets, from Lord de Tabley to Mr. Robert Nichols, there are but two references to *A Shropshire Lad*, and each time it is called the work of Mr. Laurence Housman. The mistake in the name we can afford to ignore, as it does at least keep the poems in the family, but surely it is very curious that such a book should be only referred to in passing and not discussed. *A Shropshire Lad* has been reprinted a dozen times, so that in such a detailed survey it could at least have been given some little notice, if only as popular verse— " the sort of thing the public likes." But the fact is, Mr. A. E. Housman's little volume has always been left to speak for itself, for critics have always tended to ignore it. Yet it is reprinted time after time ; it has been widely read and, I fancy, widely discussed ; its influence upon younger poets has been immense ; and it has by this time passed lightly, easily, unopposed, into our great tradition of lyrical verse. Why, then, this silence ? Has its merit always been taken for granted as something beyond dispute ? Is an acquaintance with its fine, perhaps unique, qualities and great influence assumed to be part of our general knowledge ? Or are there other, very different, reasons why it is so often passed over ? I think there are, and that they are too numerous to be tabulated here ; but a few of them are worth noticing. In the first place, there are a great many critics who are only impressed by a sheer bulk of writing ; they must be continually reminded of a writer's existence by new work, or they forget him. Those who deal largely in essay-reviews like nothing better than the appearance of book after book by names that have gradually gathered about them a safe cluster of attributes, the use of which renders the task of criticizing a contemporary as easy as that of appreciating Shakespeare and, of course, much more entertaining. Unfortunately, Mr. Housman, probably knowing nothing of this preference, comes along with an almost full-grown masterpiece, resets it once or twice, and then, only after twenty-five years have passed, produces another volume, thereby giving little opportunity for that easy talk of " still the same note, but a little more of this and a little less of the other," which carries one so comfortably to the bottom of a column. Another and more important reason for this critical neglect is concerned with the charge of " pessimism " that has been urged against these poems. There are a great many people in this country who seem to circle about literature in order that they may occasionally swoop down and carry off some morsel of comforting doctrine : they look for an inspiring message and go through a volume of verse with one eye open for tags to round off their half-hour talks to plain men ; they are generally in search of what they are pleased to call " vision," and they are apt to find it in some very strange places. Such an attitude of mind towards literature is unfortunate, but it is not, I think, quite so hopelessly wrong as the prevailing mode of criticism would have us believe ; it has at least some health in it, and that is more than can be said of some more fashionable methods of approaching letters ; but it has, of course, the serious disadvantage of encouraging cheap thought, and a shallow optimism, and of estranging those who hold it from a very fine company of writers. It has certainly made many refuse the clear but bitter draught held out to them by Mr. Housman, and so, for better or worse, we have been spared the endless comment and quotation that has fastened upon some other kinds of verse. As for the charge itself, it is too general, too vague, to be worth detailed discussion in such a brief essay as this. The whole question of the "pessimistic" poet is sufficiently tangled to be meat and drink to Mr. Chesterton himself. To say that a man is at once a poet and a pessimist is to be guilty of a contradiction in terms. Every work of art is an affirmation; your true, thoroughgoing pessimist would never think it worth while to create anything; a man without hope would never accept the labour of writing, for he could only write in the hope of being read, and surely that is almost the height of sanguine expectation. I, for one, am quite ready to lay my hand on my heart and declare that any person who is willing to take the trouble and risk of writing and publishing a volume of poems is optimistic enough for me. If—to return to *A Shropshire Lad*—it could be proved in some way that, acting under its influence, a number of young men had—let us say—committed suicide, as the over-enthusiastic disciples of Hegesias, the "orator of death," are said to have done at Alexandria, most of us would be disturbed, probably horrified, and rightly so. But even then, writing as one who sees magnificent poetry in the volume, I must confess that I should be also somewhat mystified, for the more fine poetry there is in the world the less reason there is for quitting it so hurriedly and needlessly.

There are, of course, more reasons than these why *A Shropshire Lad* has been, as it were, courted in private and shunned in public ; but it is very doubtful if they are worth finding. We, in this place, can certainly turn with more profit to the poetry itself. An analysis of the content of these hundred or so short poems is not to my present purpose, but, on the other hand, for reasons that will appear below, some notice of the poet's attitude—or, if you will, of the mood that inspired these things—seems to me absolutely essential. The poems are not, as it were, threaded on a string in either volume ; they have not that sort of unity, that dependence upon one another, which we usually find in—say—a sonnet-sequence ; but nevertheless one spirit breathes through them ; they flow out of one central mood. We cannot explain this dominating mood in terms of something outside poetry, such as a system of ethics or a definitely formulated philosophy. Judged by such alien standards, the poet is contradictory and downright perverse in his determination to make the worst of things ; thus his running grievance, on examination, can be resolved into two separate complaints that are not at all consistent ; in the first, life is lovely enough, but all too short, and death is the enemy of happiness ; in the second, existence itself is a misery only to be endured until the welcome arrival of death the deliverer. Yet when we are actually reading the poems we never feel that the poet is thus cancelling out his complaints. No, because such a contradiction (which would be very awkward if poetry were what some people think it is, philosophy in fancy dress) is not really there—indeed, has nothing to do with the actual poetry at all. In order to find it, we have to make a gigantic falsification ; we have to translate that strangely beautiful logic of the whole being of Man which we call poetry into that smaller drier logic which is simply a part of Man's intellectual apparatus. If, when engaged in the hopeless task of disentangling the myriad threads of a poem's fabric, we make references to systems of belief, schools of philosophy, and the like, we do so for the sake of mere convenience, and such references are purposely loose and vague, a mere wave of the hand towards a supposed point of the compass for a fellow-traveller's guidance.

In that fine poem *On Wenlock Edge*, we hear of the old city of Uricon and are told :

> Then, 'twas before my time, the Roman
>   At yonder heaving hill would stare :
> The blood that warms an English yoeman,
>   The thoughts that hurt him, they were there.

I seem to see that Roman lurking behind all these poems. He was, I imagine, of the early Empire, saturated in all the nobler ideas of his time, and deeply versed in its great literature—a Stoic, but one not disdainful, in some moods, of the opposite camp. (He it is who has given these lyrics, for all their English softness, that touch of iron, that suggestion of the chisel ; who has brought in the soldier, and made the lads leave their scythes rusting in the deep grass ;

who has made the volume seem one long meditation upon death. He had bided his time until the creeds were crashing down and the world was gazing blankly at the towering bleak formulas (then so hard and clear in outline, now grown so shadowy) that science had erected; this was his moment, and he took it; so that in this pretended speech of Westcountry lads and lasses, these songs of an English country-side with the " hedgerows heaped with may," we hear his many promptings, and they become clearer as the tale is told. He was not always near at hand, this Roman of ours, when the poet was writing; I fancy he knew little or nothing of such things as—

> There pass the careless people
>   That call their souls their own :
> Here by the road I loiter,
>   How idle and alone.

or better still—

> That is the land of lost content,
>   I see it shining plain,
> The happy highways where I went
>   And cannot come again.

or again, this verse, one out of many in the new volume—

> I sought them far and found them
>   The sure, the straight, the brave,
> The hearts I lost my own to,
>   The souls I could not save.
> They braced their belts about them,
>   They crossed in ships the sea,
> They sought and found six feet of ground,
>   And there they died for me.

But, on the other hand, sometimes he does more than prompt ; here and there he seems to have taken up the chisel himself in the high Roman fashion :

> Be still, my soul, be still ; the arms you bear are brittle,
>   Earth and high heaven are fixt of old and founded strong.
> Think rather, call to thought, if now you grieve a little,
>   The days when we had rest, O soul, for they were long.

Meditations upon death are nothing new to those who know their English literature. If a man of these islands has any command of style, it will not be long before he is brooding over the grave. The subject of death must be a real boon to our anthologists. But *A Shropshire Lad* wears its cypress with a difference. Not one of our poets—not even Webster, Blair, or Beddoes—has been more concerned with death than this one, who cannot write even a little song in praise of Spring without the sharp shadow falling across the sunlit blossom :

> And since to look at things in bloom
> Fifty Springs are little room,
> About the woodlands I will go
> To see the cherry hung with snow.

But most of our poets, and indeed rhetoricians, have very naturally taken the mediæval or romantic, as opposed to the classical, the Christian as opposed to the pagan, view of the matter. Seeking an image or symbol, the English imagination, essentially romantic, has always turned eagerly to the worms, skeletons, skulls, coffins, and what not of the Christian pageantry of death. A casual reader would probably declare that *A Shropshire Lad*, too, is full of such things. In reality

it is not—as anyone may see for himself. The poet
has once turned to a newer, and gone back to an
older, fashion of regarding death. Practically all the
old fantastic and frightful imagery has disappeared.
In one of the poet's moods, and particularly in the
earlier poems, we see death as the great dark curtain
against which the lovely things of life stand out
pathetically small and bright. All the lovers in
A Shropshire Lad cry out upon the piteous brevity
of life : they see only a little way before them that
house of dust where—

> Lovers lying two and two
>   Ask not whom they sleep beside,
> And the bridegroom all night through
>   Never turns him to the bride.

Our existence is but a little halt on the immeasurable
frontiers of this great country of the dead, a land
that knows nothing of either the pains of hell or the
delights of heaven ; and we have so little time to
breathe and move and feel :

> Speak now, and I will answer.
>   How shall I help you, say,
> Ere to the wind's twelve quarters
>   I take my endless way ?

And so, more recently, as he reviews the enchanted
Autumns of the earth he falls into the same mood,
tempered by more resignation and losing some of its
former urgency, and tells us to

> Possess, as I possessed a season,
>   The countries I resign. . . .

But when his mood hardens into Senecan despair of
"the embittered hour," the life of this world takes
on darker hues, and death is no longer a menace, for
it promises rest and sleep and forgetfulness :

> Now, and I muse for why and never find the reason,
>   I pace the earth, and drink the air, and feel the sun.
> Be still, be still, my soul ; it is but for a season :
>   Let us endure an hour and see injustice done.

And at times, as in a very characteristic poem in the
later volume, he will but steel himself to endure,
making no truce with either this world or the next,
the laws of God or Man ; but only making a gesture
of almost Oriental resignation :

> And how am I to face the odds
> Of Man's bedevilment and God's ?
> I, a stranger and afraid
> In a world I never made.

We have seen enough now of the mood that lie
behind these poems to know that not only is it not
the common fit of depression that it first appears,
but that it is distinctly uncommon—indeed, an
entirely individual state of mind. But the form in
which it is expressed does even more to give the
poems their unmistakable, personal note. Most of
the chief characteristics of that form will be noticed
in their turn, but before we come to speak of them it
is well that we should remark the general scheme or
design of *A Shropshire Lad*—the particular mould,
as it were, into which this molten mass of thoughts
and emotions has been poured. The book, be it
noted, is not called *Dust and Tears, Poems in Exile,*

G

The Iron Days, or anything of that kind : it is called *A Shropshire Lad.* Now Mr. Housman is, I take it, a native of the place, but I do not suppose for one moment that at the time he was composing these lyrics he always referred to himself as a Shropshire lad or asked new acquaintances to address him as such. In short, what he did in this volume was to depart from the usual practice of our modern lyric poets : instead of directly expressing his various moods he partly dramatized them in a more or less definite atmosphere, on a more or less consistent plan. By doing this he dowered his work with a certain concrete and particular effect, the success of which is one reason for its power. It might easily have proved a source of weakness, as it has done since to some poets ; it is the sureness of his touch, that mark of the artist, that has made his experiment so successful. He has been singled out and applauded as the originator of the " topographical " or " praise-the-place-where-I-was-born " manner in verse, which has become so fashionable. But the modern craze, as a mere craze, for eulogizing one's native place probably owes more to those two gentlemen who have sung of Sussex with such geniality and gusto. And we have only to think of Barnes, T. E. Brown, and Tennyson himself, to name only a few, and what they had been doing not long before, to see that setting poems in a certain definite locality and atmosphere (even to writing them in dialect, which was, I think, wisely avoided in *A Shropshire Lad*) was neither a new device nor even an old one newly

restored. It is, I repeat, his sureness of touch that
calls for our praise. For the purposes of a lyric poet,
the partial dramatization has been done to perfection.
If the poet wishes to drop the slight mask and speak
out directly in his own person, as he does here and
there, the continuity of the poems is not broken,
and we are not irritated by a demand to jump out of
one atmosphere into another. Indeed, there are all
degrees of dramatization, shading off one into another,
in these two small volumes, and in any long study it
would certainly be worth while examining them and
trying to decide what the poet has gained by adopting
so unusual a plan, gained, that is, not in this poem
or that, but in the whole mass regarded as a complete
and distinct work. What is certain to my mind is
that of all our lyric poets who have deliberately gone
to the country-side and assumed the smock-frock,
which leaves out of count poets like Burns and Clare
who had no need to go, not one has grappled with
the resulting problems more successfully than this
poet of Shropshire. With extraordinary skill and
tact, he has contrived to avoid the two pitfalls into
one or other of which most of his fellows have fallen.
Firstly, he has kept out that suggestion of the pastoral
with its Corydon and Phyllis, its perfumed sheep and
beribboned stage crooks, which we find so often in
the poetry of earlier men. Secondly, he has avoided
a mistake common to poets who have written since
A Shropshire Lad appeared—the mistake of leaving
one's artistic judgment to the mercy of certain
theories and so insisting upon one's readers admiring

the muck-heap and smelling the manure. There
was Wordsworth, of course, who managed to avoid
both these extremes, but then he contrived to dig a
special pitfall for himself, and as everyone knows
what that was, there is no need to enlarge upon it.
One would like to hear Wordsworth on *A Shropshire
Lad*. I fancy he would strongly disapprove of it,
and yet it comes nearer to one part of his famous
theory than his own work ever did. Perhaps he would
be astonished to learn that many of us who confess
to being Wordsworthians in and out of season yet
recognize in this later and lesser poet of ours an
artist, in the narrower sense, more tactful, delicate,
and scrupulous than he, the great W. W., could ever
claim to be.

Our English tongue has always favoured two
particular kinds of short poem, the single cry and the
dancing narrative, the Lyric and the Ballad. For
them it has ever been an instrument nothing short of
marvellous in its subtlety and range. It is a language
that is always ready to lilt and fall into strange and
beautiful cadences; it would be for ever on the
wing. For this very reason it has always proved itself
a difficult medium for a third kind of short poem,
which we may call the Epigram. Here is a form
that demands no flight of wings, but a chisel and the
graven stone; that asks for clearness, brevity, weight,
words frozen into miraculous phrases and not words
grown riotous, fluttering, and piping their way into
immortality. Strive as we may to create the Epigram,
the language is always against us; it will leap and

dance and sing instead of falling into beautiful attitudes. So-called epigrams, witty-pointed couplets, and quatrains, we have, of course, in plenty ; but the real epigrammatic note is rarely heard in our poetry, and when we do hear it we may be sure that something like a miracle has been wrought in the craft of verse. So far, perhaps, we deal in commonplaces ; but no matter, for what follows is no commonplace. In the poetry we are considering there can be discovered all three forms. Through the familiar supple warp and weft of Lyric and Ballad there runs the stiff and shining thread of epigram. But the metaphor is ill-chosen, for even your brocade can be unravelled, its threads disentangled and laid apart ; whereas here, in this poetic form, we have not a woven thing, but a blend, never quite the same in any two poems, yet always there, personal and unmistakable.

The influence of the ballad upon *A Shropshire Lad* is obvious, and need not detain us long. At first sight many of these poems might seem to be dreadful parodies of folk-songs. They have the same simplicity of form, the same apparently artless manner, but with a very different spirit informing them. They have the same rare qualities : high imagination and dramatic intensity governed by a fine sense of artistic reticence ; throughout there is the same strict economy of means. Such verses as these :

> My mother thinks us long away ;
>   'Tis time the field were mown.
> She had two sons at rising day,
>   To-night she'll be alone.

and

> Oh, lad, what is it, lad, that drips
>   Wet from your neck on mine ?
> What is it falling on my lips,
>   My lad, that tastes of brine ?

have the ring of the fine old ballads. Although every situation is strongly conceived, and all the resulting emotions strongly felt by the poet, yet it is mainly by the exercise of his power of compression, his artistic thrift, that he achieves such dramatic force and intensity of feeling. He does not allow an emotion to be entirely diffused by expending too many words upon it. The reader's imagination must take wing to follow the narrative in this poetry, as it must do to appreciate the old ballad literature. Thus, in that poignant lyric *Is My Team Ploughing?* all we hear are the two voices, one questioning and the other answering—the reedy cry from the grave, and the full-blooded tones of the living man. Again, in *The True Lover* there is nothing but a vague dreadful whispering in the darkness : it has the piteous appeal of such a thing as *Clerk Saunders*. But that other form, the Lyric, is naturally the basis of the whole volume. Indeed, many of its readers may be surprised that it should be necessary to go outside the Lyric to explain the peculiar charm of these poems. But such doubters have only to compare them with the work of men who were strictly singers and not gravers at all, let us say Shelley and Swinburne (but not Milton and Keats), to understand the necessity of referring to other forms. As we have seen, the expression is a curious blend, easy to recognize anywhere, but still never quite the same in any two poems. Therefore we shall not be surprised to find here and there in *A Shropshire Lad* an almost purely lyrical note :

> Loveliest of trees, the cherry now
> Is hung with bloom along the bough,
> And stands about the woodland ride
> Wearing white for Eastertide.

and

> Oh, see how thick the goldcup flowers
>   Are lying in field and lane,
> With dandelions to tell the hours
>   That never are told again.

and

> With rue my heart is laden
>   For golden friends I had,
> For many a rose-lipt maiden
>   And many a lightfoot lad.

or from the last poem of all—

> Ours were idle pleasures,
>   Yet, oh, content we were,
> The young to wind the measures,
>   The old to heed the air ;
> And I to lift with playing
>   From tree and tower and steep
> The light delaying,
>   And flute the sun to sleep.

—verses that are lovely in the old way that we know so well. But one cannot go very far without coming across that third thing, the touch of the epigram. Even some of the quotations I had selected as examples of lyrical flow began to show traces of it, and I had

to set them aside. As an instance, even in this
verse :

> Oh, tarnish late on Wenlock Edge,
>   Gold that I never see ;
> Lie long, high snowdrifts in the hedge
>   That will not shower on me.

My ear at least begins to catch a ring slightly different
from that of the verses I have already given. But the
epigrammatic note is everywhere in these octosyllabic
verses, from which everything but the bare essentials
has been cut away. Even if you are still thinking of
the epigram as some pointed witty quatrain, four
lines taken almost at random from that curious
apologia which is the last poem but one in *A Shropshire
Lad* will serve your turn very well :

> Oh many a peer of England brews
> Livelier liquor than the Muse,
> And malt does more than Milton can
> To justify God's ways to Man.

As it stands, that is a capital epigram of the ordinary
kind. But when I talk of the epigrammatic note I
am rather thinking of a certain felicity of phrase,
not, as in our great romantics, a felicity in the power
of suggestion, when a single word can open out
wonderful vistas, but one of roundness and com-
pleteness, yet with an appeal transcending that of
mere wit. It is, of course, the glory of such familiar
things as Landor's *Proud word you never spoke* or
I strove with none, or, not to disdain propaganda, his
much less familiar epigram *On seeing a hair of Lucretia
Borgia :*

Borgia, thou once were almost too august
And high for adoration ; now thou'rt dust.
All that remains of thee these plaits unfold,
Calm hair, meandering in pellucid gold.

These are epigrams proper, but the note of them
can be heard in very different forms ; the great
sonneteers all have it ; and it is here, the gift of
our Roman, quietly working miracles in *A Shropshire
Lad*. Take the last verse of that magnificent poem
To an Athlete Dying Young, and you cannot fail
to catch it :

And round that early-laurelled head
Will flock to gaze the strengthless dead,
And find unwithered on its curls
The garland briefer than a girl's.

But it is everywhere in the work of this poet, whose
power of control, whose strong feeling for artistic
reticence and thrift, notwithstanding his other rare
gifts, constitute his greatest virtue as an artist. It
has enabled him to take time and distil his thoughts
and emotions into a fine essence. It has enabled him
to cut away all wordy excrescences and, as it were,
shape his expression like a spear-head. Some people,
even some not unintelligent critics, have declared
that anyone can write this kind of poetry if he will
only take enough trouble. But such persons are
suffering from a delusion, which would quickly vanish
if they once sat down in earnest to prove they were
right. The difficulty is not in merely taking trouble,
but in knowing what kind of trouble to take : in other

words, any fool can keep on altering and altering, but to bring a piece of work nearer and nearer to perfection with every added stroke needs an artist. I fancy such mistaken notions largely come from the application of the term " polished " to literary style, for it makes people think of polishing shoes and silver, a process at once entirely dissimilar and much less difficult.

That preference for the concrete and that distrust of the abstract, which are commonly supposed to be the mark of a good poet, are very noticeable in *A Shropshire Lad*. Indeed, sometimes its author seems to keep too close to the ground, which is an error, but pardonable because it is on the right side. There is a solid earthiness in his style that can be too suggestive, at times, of a lyrical Caliban. It is this earthiness, along with his characteristic directness of style, that makes him appear positively brutal to some of his readers. He is essentially a masculine stylist, going straight to the active voice of the verb and the concrete thing, and ruthlessly divesting his style of unnecessary adjectives and woolly abstract terms. Such a line as " Clay lies still but blood's a rover " is typical of his manner. He has, indeed, made war upon the ubiquitous adjective, and concentrated upon the bare noun and verb until they have done most of the work. He has replaced the usual wearisome host of similes by a few apparently simple but astonishingly apt metaphors, and in this way he has given his style directness, force, and a certain " tang." The shortest examination of such passages as these,

chosen with no particular care because there are so
many to be found—

> His folly has not fellow,
> Beneath the blue of day.

or

> The blood that warms an English yeoman,
> The thoughts that hurt him, they were there. . . .

or again

> Before this fire of sense decay,
> This smoke of thought blow clean away. . . .

will do more than I can, beating in the air, to show his
method and exactly what it has achieved for him.
Notwithstanding his notable restraint in the use of
metaphor, simile, and figurative language generally,
his imagery, when it does come, is usually startling,
original. He loves to flash a sudden tremendous
image across one's imagination :

> 'Tis a long way further than Knighton,
> A quieter place than Clun,
> Where doomsday may thunder and lighten,
> And little t'will matter to one.

Or, again, take that audacious image in one of the
later poems on a dead friend who—

> Has woven a winter robe,
> And made of earth and sea
> His overcoat for ever,
> And wears the turning globe.

So, too, his adjectives, when they come, are not the
least of his minor felicities. Having once known
them, who could forget " the *labouring* highway,"

"the *glancing* showers," "the *coloured* counties," and "the *springing* thyme," and "yonder *heaving* hill," and similar unforeseen but happy marriages of word to word. Crowded together like this and ruthlessly torn out of their context, they may seem to point to some rather tiresome devotee of *le mot juste ;* but set in their proper places they are indeed sparkling little gems of fine writing.

There are no intricate measures in *A Shropshire Lad*, and it is clear that its author relies very little upon the charm of metre. The new volume repeats the favourite measures of the old one, and shows that the poet has no taste for metrical experiments. He is fond of the octosyllabic line and ballad measure in its simplest form. Here and there he makes clever use of a five-line stanza, which is a striking variation on the old Short Measure, the first and third lines being unrhymed and having each a redundant syllable, the second, fourth, and fifth lines rhyming together. This peculiar metrical structure gives to the fifth line of the stanza the air of being an afterthought, which is made to add considerably to the poignant force of the verses in which it is used :

> They tolled the one bell only,
>   Groom there was none to see,
> The mourners followed after,
>   And so to church went she,
>   And would not wait for me.

But throughout *A Shropshire Lad* the poet's appeal does not depend upon a highly elaborate and cunning arrangement of vowel sounds and so forth. I am writing of a poet and not a mere dauber in words, and I do not mean for one instant to imply that he has no skill in the manipulation of vowel sounds and in other technical devices. In the verse quoted above —to take the nearest example—the two " o " sounds echoing down the verse from the first line, like the chime of the bell, show us that he knows what he is about. But he is not one of our masters of verbal music. Those rapturous, infinitely beguiling phrases that linger about the ear for ever are not for him. But, nevertheless, even here he has accomplished something that not only increases our admiration, but makes his work a fruitful study for other poets. In his moments of passionate stress he has given us, within that terse and finely tempered style of his, the true ring and cadence of ordinary natural speech. A comparison—not of the odious kind—will perhaps throw some light on a matter that is difficult to explain in a few words. Another poet of our time, Mr. W. B. Yeats, has always laboured, and on the whole successfully, to give his style a similar directness and naturalness, but at the same time he has always pursued a delicate research of his own into the endless possibilities of stressed language, so that all his best poems move to lovely little tunes of his own, which must be caught before the peculiar beauty of his work can be appreciated. So, too, all Mr. Walter de la Mare's finest things have their own music, come out in that exquisite stammer of his, and this too must be caught on the very threshold of appreciation. One would not, of course, have these two fine poets any different : they express themselves to our admiration. But this lovely personal music is not to be found in *A Shropshire Lad ;* in its place, within the simple metrical framework, is that cadence of our common human speech which no ear can help recognizing and no heart can reject. Take it at its very simplest :

> We still had sorrows to lighten—
> One could not always be glad ;
> And lads knew trouble at Knighton
> When I was a Knighton lad. . . .

Now, that is apparently as plain and straightforward as prose, but, print it as you like, you cannot make it into prose ; if you simply say the lines you must sing them, and if, on the other hand, you begin by singing them your voice must inevitably fall into their natural affecting cadence. It is this that makes his mournful folk seem to cry from the heart, as few others do in the poetry of our time. And though *A Shropshire Lad* has had such a great influence, though traces of that influence can be discovered in all manner of unlikely places in contemporary verse, I know only one or two of our younger poets who have been able to reproduce this curious characteristic. But perhaps too many of them are now more concerned with the look of a poem on the printed page than with their reader's ear.

Affirmative statements are the necessities of criticism, negative statements only its luxuries. It may be entertaining to be told the hundred-and-one things that a work of art is *not*, but it is not strictly necessary.

But if one declares that So-and-so's poetry has such and such fine qualities, and contents oneself with doing that, there are some people who are always ready to think that one has dowered So-and-so with every virtue known to letters, who are quick to protest that So-and-so is not a Homer or a Shakespeare. Solely, then, for the benefit of such persons, who are to be found even in the best company, let me cross to the other, the negative, side and declare what, in my opinion, is not to be found in Mr. Housman's poetry. It knows nothing of those supreme moments that are only to be met with in some half-dozen of our poets ; it has not those brief spells when poetry suddenly becomes sheer magic, and the poet himself nothing less than a wizard ; and it is never possessed by that consuming rapture that is perhaps the innermost secret of Shelley ; nor has it any great range and scope, or that power of transmuting all life into poetry which is the majestic glory of the greatest poets. Compared with their wide domains, it is nothing but a little estate. But it is a little estate that is exquisitely ordered. And, to turn once more to words that I have been compelled to use again and again in this brief discussion, there is in it something distinct, individual, personal. It is easy to write verse that is highly novel but not worth reading, as so many people do ; it is not very difficult to write verse that is quite readable but not original, as many others do ; but to create lyrics that have certain rare literary qualities and, further, have their creator's personality clearly stamped on them, is to have some kinship with the great masters. A line from A. E. Housman is as unmistakable as a line from Milton, Shelley, or Wordsworth, and bears the same impress of the poet's individuality ; and to me the difference between the modern poet and these three Titans, on this count of original force, is one of degree alone, for I hold him to be of the same imperishable kind.

MR. W. W. JACOBS

IF Mr. W. W. Jacobs' stories had been concerned with absinthe and prostitution instead of beer and matrimony; if they had first appeared in the *Pale Review* instead of the *Strand Magazine*, and had been afterwards brought out in small private editions instead of such-and-such a sevenpenny or shilling series; if, in short, they had succeeded in depressing a handful instead of amusing a multitude of readers, then the very persons who never mention Mr. Jacobs would long ago have called him a great artist. Delicate appreciations of his art would have made their appearance in our English literary journals, and superior persons in America, following their usual custom, would have produced thesis after thesis analysing his technique. Actually, Mr. Jacobs is not, of course, a great artist, but, nevertheless, he is an artist, and now that he has entertained us for so long, there is perhaps no danger in calling him one. No doubt most capable readers have long since recognized this fact, but they do not seem to have thought it a subject worth discussion, and in all probability simply because Mr. Jacobs happens to be very popular. Literary conditions are becoming so topsy-turvy that popularity is almost a short cut to critical oblivion: it is as if the critics and the railway-bookstall clerks

had agreed to divide contemporary literature between
them and not encroach upon each other's territory.
Of this popularity there can be no question ; it began
with the publication of his first book, nearly thirty
years ago, and it is not yet at an end. If, as Coleridge
(who would modify his statement if he lived to-day)
once remarked, an author can be said to have achieved
fame when his books are to be found in obscure
country inns, then Mr. Jacobs is indeed famous. We
have found him in the remotest little inns and have
blessed the kindly or forgetful traveller that left
him there ; we have pounced upon him in the book-
shelves of spare bedrooms here, there, and everywhere ; the night-watches have often found us
listening to the night-watchman ; Ginger Dick, Peter
Russet, and old Sam Small have gone with us and
" fleeted the time " on the longest railway journeys ;
and we have sneaked into the company of the old
man at the " Cauliflower," and Bob Pretty and the
rest, many a time when our reputations, bank-balances,
and families demanded that we should be otherwise
engaged. For my own part, I am ready to confess
that I could not name more than one-third of our
author's volumes and could not say which story is
in which volume, and yet I must have read most of
his stories over and over again at odd times, and am
quite ready to read them all over again. Mr. Jacobs
has no message for the age ; he has not imagined any
Utopias, nor even invented a new religion ; he has
not helped to solve any of our more urgent problems,
except that of obtaining liquid refreshment at a

minimum of cost; no transatlantic critic has yet
written an essay on the " Something-ism of Jacobs,"
comparing him with Strindberg and Wedekind; and
yet he need not despair. He has the satisfaction of
knowing that he has only to leave one of his volumes
in the same room with any normal English-speaking
person, and that person, opening the book and coming
across some such beginning as this :

> " Strength and good-nature "—said the night-watchman,
> musingly, as he felt his biceps—" strength and good-nature
> always go together. Sometimes you find a strong man who is
> not good-natured ; but then, as everybody he comes in contack
> with is, it comes to the same thing.
> " The strongest and kindest-'earted man I ever come across
> was a man o' the name of Bill Burton, a shipmate of Ginger
> Dick's. For that matter 'e was a shipmate o' Peter Russet's
> and old Sam Small's too. . . ."

will be compelled to settle himself (and perhaps herself) down, neglect his business, and read and enjoy
to the end. And at the end, such a reader, hurrying
to take up the threads of business again, will not find
the world a worse place than it appeared to him when
he began ; his wits will have been sharpened, and he
will have been mellowed and heartened by laughter.
Certainly, Mr. Jacobs, perched though he is on the
dubious heights of popularity, need not despair.

The few little notices of Mr. Jacobs one has seen
here and there have always pointed out that his
youth was spent in the neighbourhood of the London
docks, and the writers would seem to imagine that by
hanging about the waterside and keeping his ears
open, a man can almost automatically become the

author of *Many Cargoes* and *Odd Craft*. Clearly this will not do. Mr. Jacobs' knowledge of sailors and the seafaring life in general has obviously played its part in his authorship, but it does not explain him. Mr. Conrad and Mr. H. M. Tomlinson, I take it, know a great deal about the sea and the docks, but they are no more capable of writing, say, *The Skipper's Wooing* than Mr. Jacobs is of writing *Nostromo* or *London River*. One writer, talking about the way in which he used to meet our author occasionally at literary gatherings in the late 'nineties, remarks : " Obviously the men and women that he met on these occasions were of little use to him in his stories. Not one of us understood the difference between a barque and a schooner ; we knew something about Guy de Maupassant and Flaubert, but nothing about marline-spikes or capstans. Where W. W. Jacobs got his intricate nautical knowledge from I know not. He never paraded it : he never said ' Avast there ' or ' Shiver my timbers ' " . . . But Mr. Jacobs is not a Clark Russell with a little comedy added, and it is quite possible that in order to appreciate him to the full it is more important to know something about Maupassant than it is to know something about a marline-spike. Actually, only about one-half of his stories deal with the adventures of sailormen, and even then the adventures usually take place ashore ; while the rest have nothing whatever to do with the sea, though for the most part they find their characters in classes not far removed from that of the common sailor. Among this latter group is that series, spreading from volume to volume, which is supposed to be told to successive travellers by the old man (that adept at obtaining drink and tobacco at other people's expense without any apparent loss of dignity) at the " Cauliflower Inn " at Claybury, that series which might be called the epic of Bob Pretty, most ingenious of village rascals. I would not willingly alienate any fellow-enthusiast's sympathies at the outset by a too rash assertion of my own preferences; but I am not sure that these Bob Pretty stories are not among the very best things that Mr. Jacobs has done. Who could forget, having once read, that episode of the Prize Hamper, when the great Bob not only succeeded in winning the hamper, but also managed to obtain its value in money as well from the unsuccessful competitors; or that of the poaching, when the keepers rescued nothing more than a sack of cabbages from the middle of a very cold and muddy pond; or that encounter between Bob and the unfortunate conjurer who tried to do the famous watch trick?

These frequent references to the sea are important because they tend to show that Mr. Jacobs, when he has been approached at all by criticism, has been approached from the wrong direction. He has actually been mistaken for a realist. Such writers probably imagine that captains of small coasting vessels, when they come ashore, are immediately plunged into the most astonishing and farcical intrigues involving an imaginary rich uncle from New Zealand and what not; that a pint or two of ale given to any lighterman or bargee will result in funny tales of plot and counterplot that only need a touch here and there to make them into the most delicious short stories. But not only is Mr. Jacobs not a reporter, but an artist ; he is also, in his own way, a most finished, conscientious and delicate artist. He is himself such a master of craft that if you take from him nearly everything that usually goes with his work, that is, his humour, his dexterity in certain kinds of comic dialogue and narrative, his knowledge of the habits and the point of view of certain classes, if you take away all this, he will yet produce an excellent short story of quite a different kind. He has not a sufficiently poetic mind, not enough acquaintance with those borderland states of the human spirit, to write a horror story of the highest class, but, nevertheless, in *The Monkey's Paw*, and some other similar things, he has done very well. This incomplete but sufficiently astonishing success in work so far removed from that which we usually associate with his name must be largely set down to the credit of his technique ; it is one proof of his mastery of form. And it is this, along with his very fine sense of humour, that has made him the excellent short-story writer he is, so that any reference to particularly favourable opportunities for observing and reporting will not explain him. It is worth recollecting that at the time Mr. Jacobs began writing definitely localized fiction was becoming the fashion ; every new novelist had to have his own particular district ; London was being cut and carved and slices of it were being served out to ambitious young writers. Mr. Zangwill was given the Jewish quarters, Mr. Morrison took the East End, Mr. Pett Ridge claimed the suburbs, and so on ; thus it fell out that Mr. Jacobs, having written a few stories of seafaring men, was presented with Wapping, Rotherhithe, and the docks. This part of the world, with the addition of a few sleepy little coast towns, his Sunwich Ports, and the village of Claybury, served its purpose as a kind of map reference to the setting of his stories ; but actually, like most original writers, he was soon busily engaged creating a world of his own.

Comedy demands a world of its own. The merest hint of war, famine, or pestilence would shatter, say, a story by Jane Austen, and so she took care to create a world in which the visit of somebody's niece or the engagement of the neighbouring vicar is an event of the highest importance. Mr. Jacobs presents us with a world just as small, bright, and artificial as that of Jane Austen. Knowing exactly what he wanted to do, the kind of effect he wanted to make, he took away and refashioned the slender stock of material necessary for his setting, and boldly left out all the rest, all the darker crimes, the devastating passions, the bleak tragedies that are found everywhere in this world and that would have shattered his tiny comedies into minute fragments. To leave out so much in this fashion may seem easy, but actually it is very difficult, demanding, as artificial comedy always does, a nice taste and great tact on the part of the artist. As an example of Mr. Jacobs' delicate discrimination we need only take his treatment of that mainspring of action in life and literature, love. Love, which spins the plot here in many of these stories just as it does elsewhere, is not a passion at all with Mr. Jacobs, but merely a desire for (or sense of) possession, leading to comic rivalries during courtship and comic jealousies after marriage ; the merest glimmer of sentiment is sufficient ; and he usually contrives to end his little comedies of courtship in some such fashion as this :

He turned after a short distance for a last look at the house, and, with a sudden sense of elation, saw that she was standing on the step. He hesitated, and then walked slowly back.

" Yes ? " said Prudence.

" I should like to tell your mother that I am sorry," he said in a low voice.

" It is getting late," said the girl softly ; " but, if you really wish to tell her, Mrs. Porter will not be here to-morrow night."

which tells us that all is well with the young couple. If we are sentimentally inclined, we may allow our imaginations to brood over them, but Mr. Jacobs has retired from the stage for the little comedy is ended. All this is as it should be ; a single sentence by Mr. D. H. Lawrence would be a monster in such surroundings and would ruin everything ; Mr. Jacobs contrives with exquisite skill. It is worth remarking, however, that his treatment of love, like his treatment of other important matters, though it is primarily dictated by his limited form of art, does follow in its details the kind of life that is supposed to be treated in these stories. In other words, the comic rivalries and jealousies we get here are the kind of comic rivalries and jealousies we should expect to discover

among sailors and their people about the docks.
Realism does not break in, but it is allowed to enter,
art having posted its guards and sentries all over the
place. This is true of the general setting, and it is
true of the action and the dialogue as well; they all
represent a useful working compromise between
realism, the representation of things as they ordinarily
appear, and a deliberate, highly self-conscious art,
anxious only to achieve certain effects that things
as they are never seem to bring off neatly; but it is
a compromise like those that married couples are
often said to arrive at, one in which the lady, art,
has most of her own way.

This world of Mr. Jacobs, which is not unlike a
tiny part of the Dickens world all cleaned up, painted,
and burnished, is a very pleasant one indeed, so pleasant
as a background to our imagination that some of the
pleasure we get from these stories is nothing more nor
less than the poetical pleasure we always get from
what is called " atmosphere." It is a little world from
which all the darker shades have been banished, a
world filled with sleepy little ports, tiny coasting
vessels, trim cottages that usually have a rose-garden
or " a small, brick-paved yard, in which trim myrtles
and flowering plants stand about in freshly ochred
pots " and perhaps " neatly grained shutters and
white steps and polished brass knockers," happy little
taverns (" an old-world bar, with its loud-ticking
clock, its Windsor chairs, and its cracked jug full of
roses "), pretty, saucy girls with a string of admirers,
comic policemen, love-lorn intriguing third mates,

henpecked sea-captains, and philosophical night-watchmen. Here, in this bright limited world, with all its properties ready to be set on the stage in a few seconds, at once false and true, and certainly very English, is a delightful setting for comedy. Into this setting Mr. Jacobs projects what we may call farces, for we must now pass from setting to plot, and Mr. Jacobs' plots, the bare action of his little stories, for the most part belong to the realm of stage farce. There is an ingenious little plan to deceive some one or other, a great many lies are told, and then in the end, as a rule, the biter himself is bitten. Very often the plan involves an imaginary wealthy uncle or a mythical long-lost son, or, if not these, then either a legacy, a fortune-teller, a pretended deed of heroism, or a comic feud with the police. And nearly always these little plots of his are fantastic, artificial, and deliberately, shall we say, standardized, so that once we are in the Jacobs world we know exactly what kind of queer action people will take. A summary of one or two of the stories will do more to show the character of the action than pages of explanation. Thus, an impudent second officer, walking ashore, spies a very pretty girl, and learns that she and her mother, a widow, live alone, and also that she had a brother who went to sea many years before and never returned. Having learned this and a few other particulars, the young man boldly marches up to the door and announces himself as the long-lost brother and son. His impudence carries him through at first, but he is asked to call again, and when he does so, a huge woman, the charwoman of the house, promptly rushes in and claims him as her long-lost husband. The women have won the day. Again, two young men, one a dashing sergeant and the other a rather staid civilian, are rivals for the hand of a girl who has a taste for heroes. Her father, who wishes his daughter to marry the civilian, persuades the latter that his best plan is to save some one from drowning (the sergeant cannot swim), and, in order to make sure there is some one to save, to push his rival into the water when they are all strolling along the quay on the following Sunday afternoon. The plan is accepted, but actually it is the father himself who is pushed into the water and saved from drowning, and his subsequent conduct, in its seeming ingratitude, comes in for a good deal of comment. Again, there is the strong man whom the night-watchman was on the point of introducing to us above ; he who was amazingly powerful, but very sociable and good-humoured. Unfortunately, when he went out with Ginger Dick and the rest, he would never touch beer, which he said had a bad effect upon him, but only such slops as lemonade. Finally, however, his friends persuaded him to drink as they did, and the unhappy sequel was that he proved to be very nasty indeed in liquor, giving them all a good hiding and creating an uproar wherever he went. The following day, Ginger Dick and the other, not relishing his companionship, tell him that a certain landlord he encountered the night before is dying from the effect of his boisterous social methods. This ruse, however, only makes a desperate man of him, and he proceeds to further his chances of escaping by tying up his friends one by one as they come into the room, and going off with their money. This is farce worked out like neat little problems in algebra.

But the plot, that is, the main lines of the action, the central situation, is not the story. If it were, we should have grown tired of Mr. Jacobs years ago. His humour seems to demand plots of this kind, but they are only the beginning. Any second or third-rate humorist could invent such situations, which are the stock-in-trade of the confirmed writer of farces and the terror of the playgoer; and if they are to be transformed into something rich, if not strange, a Jacobs is necessary. These things are artificial, as artificial as Restoration Comedy; but now there enters Mr. Jacobs, the comic realist, who pours into these common, though quaint little vessels, his own rich bubbling brew, an essence distilled from Wapping and Rotherhithe, though we may admit that it is a sublimated Wapping, a glorified Rotherhithe. The result is something that is not mere farce on the one hand, nor the mere realistic humorous " sketch " on the other, but an art that makes use of both and transcends them, a kind of midsummer night-watchman's dream. The atmosphere is that of Wapping, and the talk seems as natural to the speakers as grass in the field:

Sailormen don't bother much about their relations as a rule, said the night-watchman; sometimes because a railway-ticket costs as much as a barrel o' beer, and they ain't got the money for both, and sometimes because most relations run away with the idea that a sailorman has been knocking about 'arf over the world just to bring them 'ome presents.

Then, agin, some relations are partikler about appearances, and they don't like it if a chap don't wear a collar and tidy 'imself up. Dress is everything nowadays ; put me in a top-'at and tail-coat, with a twopenny smoke stuck in my mouth, and who would know the difference between me and a lord ? Put a bishop in my clothes, and you'd ask 'im to 'ave a 'arf-pint as soon as you would me—sooner, p'r'aps.

Yet the way in which every situation is fully exploited and the point and finish of the dialogue are in the very best traditions of comedy, the comedy that sees itself on a stage even though it may be written in a book. A random dip into these volumes takes us into the company of Mr. Gunnill, who is talking with his daughter :

"Bailed out," said Miss Gunnill, in a deep and thrilling voice ; "bailed out at one o'clock in the morning, brought home singing loud enough for half a dozen, and then talking about flowers ! "

Mr. Gunnill coughed again.

"I was dreaming," pursued Miss Gunnill, plaintively, "sleeping peacefully, when I was awoke by a horrible noise."

"That couldn't ha' been me," protested her father. "I was only a bit cheerful. It was Benjamin Ely's birthday yesterday, and after we left the Lion they started singing, and I just hummed to keep 'em company. It wasn't singing, mind you, only humming—when up comes that interfering Cooper and takes me off."

Miss Gunnill shivered, and with her pretty cheek in her hand, sat by the window the very picture of despondency. "Why didn't he take the others ? " she inquired.

"*Ah !* " said Mr. Gunnill, with great emphasis, "that's what a lot more of us would like to know. P'r'aps if you'd been more polite to Mrs. Cooper, instead o' putting it about that she looked young enough to be his mother, it wouldn't have happened."

His daughter shook her head impatiently and, on Mr. Gunnill making an allusion to breakfast, expressed surprise that he had got the heart to eat anything. Mr. Gunnill pressing the point, however, she arose and began to set the table, the undue care with which she smoothed out the creases of the tablecloth, and the mathematical exactness with which she placed the various articles, all being so many extra smarts in his wound. When she finally placed enough food for a dozen people he began to show signs of a little spirit.

" Ain't you going to have any ? " he demanded, as Miss Gunnill resumed her seat by the window.

" *Me ?* " said the girl, with a shudder. " Breakfast ? The disgrace is breakfast enough for me. I couldn't eat a morsel ; it would choke me."

Mr. Gunnill eyed her over the rim of his teacup. " I come down an hour ago," he said casually, as he helped himself to some bacon.

Miss Gunnill started despite herself. " Oh ! " she said, listlessly.

" And I see you making a very good breakfast all by yourself in the kitchen," continued her father, in a voice not free from the taint of triumph.

The discomfited Selina rose and stood regarding him ; Mr. Gunnill, after a vain attempt to meet her gaze, busied himself with his meal.

" The idea of watching every mouthful I eat ! " said Miss Gunnill tragically ; " the idea of complaining because I have some breakfast ! I'd never have believed it of you, never ! st's shameful ! Fancy grudging your own daughter the food she eats ! "

Eventually, Mr. Gunnill is fined ten shillings and lectured by the magistrate, much to his annoyance :

His feelings against Police Constable Cooper increased with the passing of the days. The constable watched him with the air of a proprietor, and Mrs. Cooper's remark that " her husband had had his eye upon him for a long time, and that he had better be careful for the future," was faithfully retailed to him within half an hour of its utterance. Convivial friends counted his cups for him ; teetotal friends more than hinted that Cooper was in the employ of his good angel.

Miss Gunnill's two principal admirers had an arduous task to perform. They had to attribute Mr. Gunnill's disaster to the vindictiveness of Cooper, and at the same time to agree with his daughter that it served him right. Between father and daughter they had a difficult time, Mr. Gunnill's sensitiveness having been much heightened by his troubles.

" Cooper ought not to have taken you," said Herbert Sims, for the fiftieth time.

" He must ha' seen you like it dozens o' times before," said Ted Drill, who, in his determination not to be outdone by Mr. Sims, was not displaying his usual judgment. " Why didn't he take you then ? That's what you ought to have asked the magistrate."

" I don't understand you," said Mr. Gunnill, with an air of cold dignity.

" Why," said Mr. Drill, " what I mean is—look at that night for instance, when——"

He broke off suddenly, even his enthusiasm not being proof against the extraordinary contortions of visage in which Mr. Gunnill was indulging.

" When ? " prompted Selina and Mr. Sims together. Mr. Gunnill, after first daring him with his eye, followed suit.

" That night at the Crown," said Mr. Drill, awkwardly. " You know ; when you thought that Joe Gaggs was the landlord. You tell 'em ; you tell it best. I've roared over it."

" I don't know what you're driving at," said the harassed Mr. Gunnill bitterly.

" H'm ! " said Mr. Drill, with a weak laugh. " I've been mixing you up with somebody else."

Mr. Gunnill, obviously relieved, said that he ought to be more careful, and pointed out, with some feeling, that a lot of mischief was caused that way.

These two quotations are interesting because they show that Mr. Jacobs' humour is by no means dependent upon a farcical situation ; in this particular story there is a very funny situation indeed, involving two helmets and two truncheons and an irate policeman ; but it has not yet come in sight, and yet there is so much humour by the way, in what would be for most short-story writers the mere expository part of the tale.

Even when we have read one of these stories several times and could relate off-hand the whole train of events described in it, we can still read it again with pleasure simply because of the humour in the dialogue and the suggestive little flashes of description. I have seen it stated somewhere that Mr. Jacobs derives his humour from that of Smollett and Dickens ; but this is a superficial criticism, and, like most superficial criticisms, it is unjust to everybody concerned in it. Smollett deals in externals ; his humour is compact of horseplay and odd appearances ; Dickens, carrying on from Smollett, began by describing horseplay and odd figures, but very quickly raised English humour to a height it had not reached since Shakespeare by the creation of richly comic characters who are themselves almost inexhaustible storehouses of absurdity. The humour of Mr. Jacobs, however, has neither the rude vigour of the first nor the imaginative richness of the second ; it is limited, neat, finished ; and, actually, it is a different kind of humour altogether, the humour of a witty dramatist, out to exploit a situation rather than a character, and achieving its end by verbal dexterity rather than by the absurdities of a poetic, extravagant, comic imagination. Sam Weller, who is not a typical Dickens comic character, being a conscious wit and not an unconscious absurdity, like, say, Micawber, is probably the only Dickens figure of any importance that might easily remind us of the Jacobs people. When Dickens created Weller he probably did what Mr. Jacobs seems to have done all along, that is, he took the average cockney humorist of the street and carefully heightened the wit and point of his talk. Much of the humour in these stories is discovered in little gems of talk that we feel we might have picked up from any taproom had we haunted the place long enough. But we should have to haunt it a long, long time before we overheard things as good as these :

The tap-room was crowded that night, but we all 'ad to pay threepence each—coining money, I call it. Some o' the things wot 'e done was very clever ; but a'most from the start-off there was unpleasantness. When 'e asked somebody to lend 'im a pocket-'ankercher to turn into a white rabbit, Henery Walker rushed up and lent 'im 'is, but instead of a white rabbit it turned into a black one with two white spots on it, and arter Henery Walker 'ad sat for some time puzzling over it 'e got up and went off 'ome without saying good-night to a soul.

Or a typical remark by the night-watchman, that master of the art of innuendo :

I got to know about it through knowing the servant that lived there. A nice, quiet gal she was, and there wasn't much went on that she didn't hear. I've known 'er to cry for hours with the ear-ache, pore gal. . . .

a remark that occurs at the beginning of a tale called *Dixon's Return*, which is not strictly a comic story,

I

and yet is one of the best stories that Mr. Jacobs has ever written, being one of those supremely satisfying tales of a worm that turned. Dixon was the owner of a pub, who was dreadfully bullied by his wife and her relatives and finally ran away to sea, not being heard of for years. When he returned, he pretended to be as meek and mild as ever; but finding that they were all just as ready to bully him as they were before, he asserted himself manfully, kicked his blustering cousins out of the place and had a few words with his lady, who was never the same again:

Of all the nice-mannered, soft-spoken landladies I've ever seen, she was the best, and on'y to 'ear the way she answered her 'usband when he spoke to 'er was a pleasure to every married man in the bar.

Here is a characteristic touch that we find everywhere in these stories:

" I married agin," ses Peter's uncle, in a whisper, 'cos people was telling 'im to keep quiet, " a tartar—a perfect tartar. She's in a 'orsepittle at present, else I shouldn't ha' been able to come if I 'adn't found five pounds wot she's hid in a matchbox up the chimbley."

" But wot'll you do when she finds it out ? " ses Sam, opening 'is eyes.

" I'm going to 'ave the house cleaned and the chimbleys swept to welcome 'er 'ome," ses Mr. Goodman, taking a sip o' whisky. " It'll be a little surprise for her."

And here is another, one of those effective pieces of stage dialogue we often find in Mr. Jacobs' work:

The solicitor sniffed. " I could write tract after tract on temperance," he said bitterly. " I wonder what our poor wives are thinking? I expect they have put us down as dead."

"Crying their eyes out," said the doctor wistfully; "but they'll dry them precious quick when we get back, and ask all sorts of questions. What are you going to say, Harry?"

"The truth," said the solicitor virtuously.

"So am I," said his friend; "but mind, we must both tell the same tale, whatever it is. . . ."

Sometimes a mere phrase will heighten an absurd situation almost beyond belief. Thus, in that story in which a rather mean young man, one George Wright, persuades an old sailor, Mr. Kemp, to take the part of an imaginary rich uncle from New Zealand, in order to impress his girl and her mother—the whole fun is that, once embarked on the scheme, the stingy young man has to give his fellow-conspirator pounds and pounds to keep up the illusion of vast wealth; and a single phrase crowns the situation delightfully:

Mr. Kemp obeyed, and the following evening, after sitting a little while chatting in the shop, was invited into the parlour, where, mindful of Mr. Wright's instructions, he held his listeners enthralled by tales of past expenditure. A tip of fifty pounds to his bedroom steward coming over was characterised by Mrs. Bradshaw as extravagant.

"Seems to be going all right," said Mr. Wright, as the old man made his report; "but be careful; don't go overdoing it."

Mr. Kemp nodded. "I can turn 'em round my little finger," he said. "You'll have Bella all to yourself to-morrow evening."

Mr. Wright flushed. "How did you manage that?" he inquired. "It's the first time she has ever been out with me alone."

"She ain't coming out," said Mr. Kemp. "She's going to stay at home and mind the shop; it's the mother what's coming out. Going to spend the evening with me."

Mr. Wright frowned. "What did you do that for?" he demanded hotly.

"I didn't do it," said Mr. Kemp equably; "they done it. The old lady says that, just for once in her life, she wants to see how it feels to spend money like water."

"*Money like water!*" repeated the horrified Mr. Wright. . . .

And there we may leave them. But I cannot leave off quoting before I plunder something from what I have always regarded as Mr. Jacobs' best story, *The Money Box*, from an early volume entitled *Odd Craft*. Ginger Dick and Peter Russet, having grown tired of spending their money quickly, arrange that their pay shall be given to a fellow-seaman, old Isaac Lunn, a very steady old teetotaller, and that he shall live with them ashore and give it to them bit by bit:

Anybody but Ginger Dick and Peter Russet or a fool would ha' known better than to do such a thing, but old Isaac 'ad got such a oily tongue and seemed so fair-minded about what 'e called moderate drinking that they never thought wot they was letting themselves in for, and when they took their pay—close on sixteen pounds each—they put the odd change in their pocket and handed over the rest to him.

The first day they was as pleased as Punch. Old Isaac got a nice, respectable bedroom for them all, and arter they'd 'ad a few drinks they humoured 'im by 'aving a nice 'ot cup 'o tea, and then goin' off with 'im to see a magic-lantern performance.

It was called "The Drunkard's Downfall," and it begun with a young man going into a nice-looking pub and being served by a nice-looking barmaid with a glass of ale. Then it got on to 'arf-pints and pints in the next picture, and arter Ginger 'a seen the lost young man put away six pints in about 'arf a minute, 'e got such a raging thirst on 'im that 'e couldn't sit still, and 'e whispered to Peter Russet to go out with 'im.

"You'll lose the best if you go now," ses old Isaac, in a

whisper ; " in the next picture there's little frogs and devils sitting on the edge of the pot as 'e goes to drink."

Ginger Dick got up and nodded to Peter.

" Arter that 'e kills 'is mother with a razor," ses old Isaac, pleading with 'im and 'olding on to 'is coat.

Ginger Dick sat down agin, and when the murder was over 'e said it made 'im feel faint, and 'im and Peter Russet went out for a breath of fresh air. They 'ad three at the first place, and then they moved on to another and forgot all about Isaac and the dissolving views until ten o'clock, when Ginger, who 'ad been very liberal to some friends 'e made in a pub, found 'e'd spent 'is last penny. . . .

The tangle of events that follows, how the old man outwitted the enraged Ginger and Peter, and did not return their money to them until they were all out to sea again, all these things are known to those who have read the story (and they will surely want to read it again now), and may be discovered by those who have not read it within the covers of *Odd Craft*. The latter, if they have any humour themselves, living in days when all fiction seems to be drifting into the hands either of poor potboilers or of humorless geniuses who are filled with half-digested notions and will not take any pains with their matter, will rejoice to find a genuine humorist who has no views to thrust down their throats, who has taken trouble with his work and entertained us without any fuss for years. And they will join the rest of us in offering him our thanks.

MR. ROBERT LYND: ESSAYIST

NOWADAYS it is too often assumed that literary genius is always to be found " apart sat on a hill retired," labouring at some new form that will not be appreciated by the common run of men for at least two generations. We even go so far as to forget that though a man who uses some literary form that the public does not want may possibly be a genius, he may possibly be nothing of the kind, may be nothing better than a conceited ass. This comes of brooding overmuch upon exotic and revolutionary talents, and taking the others for granted. The others are those men of rich mind and ample energy who have been so much in love with literature that they have simply taken the form that was lying in their way, the five-act drama in blank verse, the rambling novel, the periodical essay, and raised it into a fit instrument of their genius. As Mr. Chesterton once remarked : " Minor poets cannot write to order ; but very great poets can write to order. The larger the man's mind, the wider his scope of vision, the more likely it will be that anything suggested to him will seem significant and promising ; the more he has a grasp of everything, the more ready he will be to write anything." To be able to make the ascent of Parnassus part of the day's work, frankly to accept the common worn coins of the market-place and then, by some mysterious means, to transform them into new bright mintage, this is the mark only of a man of full-blooded talent, a man opulently gifted, one, if only a fledgling, of the Shakespearean brood. The point need not be laboured, but it must be made, for it happens that Mr. Robert Lynd, one of the best miscellaneous prose writers of our generation, an essayist of rare charm, an acute, witty, yet tolerant critic, is a journalist. Moreover, he is a very good journalist, not one of those men of letters who with a great show of disdain merely boil their pots in Fleet Street and can hardly bring themselves to endorse the cheques they receive from newspapers ; but a real journalist and one so magnificently equipped that any editor, not a fool or a red-hot Tory, would welcome him with delight. In his time Mr. Lynd has probably done most things that can be done on either a newspaper or a weekly review, and it is certain that he can write any feature of the literary side of a paper, whether it is a piece of descriptive writing, a short article or a book review, better than almost anyone else. The mere fact of having to be topical, of being compelled to write about something merely because it happened yesterday, is in itself sufficient to dry up the source of wit and fancy in a great many literary men, but this necessity only seems to stimulate Mr. Lynd. No matter where he is sent (if he is sent), he returns in triumph, waving the brush. His descriptive writing, for example, is magnificent journalism, prompt to the occasion and ready to dance any reader's eye down to the bottom of a newspaper column; but even at its lightest it is also something more than journalism, for there is a quality in it that will withstand the lapse of a day or a month or a year. We have only to glance at his account of a visit to the Derby and of a night's boxing, two pieces of descriptive writing that were done for a daily paper, to see that even the most ferocious newspaperman would applaud them as journalism; but we should also discover in the first, passages like this:

Then one had a glimpse of three horses close—well, fairly close—on each other's tails, and none of them the grey Tetratema. I noticed that on one of them crouched a jockey in exquisite grass-green. He passed like a fine phrase out of a poem of which one does not know the rest.

And notice that the second opened in this fashion:

You haven't the slightest idea what a great boxing-match looks like, now that it takes place in a special sort of light in order that it may be photographed for the picture theatres. The ring under its roof of lamps looks partly like a billiard table. It looks still more like the stage just before the ghost in *Hamlet* appears.

You could not imagine a more eerie and lavender light. If it were freezing in Elsinore, and not a mouse stirring, it could scarcely produce a more moonstruck or ghostly atmosphere ...

and we should have to confess that even in its easiest strain there is an imaginative quality in his writing that makes it rise superior to the hand-to-mouth work of journalism.

Mr. Lynd then, instead of preening himself in a

corner, has done what so many of our eighteenth-
century writers did : he has marched into literature
by way of journalism, the day's round, the common
task. It is not everybody's way, but it is especially
suitable for writers with well-stored, sane, and masculine minds, men who can take hold of experience
and translate it freely, who can ransack their own
minds and plunder the outside world with an equal
measure of success ; and when once a man does
enter literature by this road, there can be no doubt
as to his capacity ; he is worth hearing. While Mr.
Lynd has been proving to all good judges that he is
one of the ablest literary journalists of our time, he
has also been creating for himself a singularly happy
position in the literature of our time. Some people
consider this antithesis of literature and journalism
entirely false, and declare that there is, or (sometimes)
ought to be, no difference between the two. But in
reply, taking the matter in its simplest form, we can
point out that books (even bad books) are still produced with an eye to permanency and for the ultimate
benefit of posterity, and papers are still produced
with an eye to the moment and for the ultimate
benefit of the fishmonger ; that journalism, unlike
literature, does not pretend to stand by itself, but has
to depend on its topical appeal, its value as news
(even a review is simply news of a book) ; that the
mere fact that some, a few, writers have succeeded
in both forms, have sometimes bridged the gulf, only
proves that there is a gulf to bridge and accentuates
the difference between the two forms. If the other

side could produce a long list of writers who are given an equally uproarious welcome by newspaper editors and fastidious literary critics, then our case would be considerably weakened. But no such long list will be forthcoming; it will be a very short list, and prominent among the few names on it will be that of Mr. Lynd.

Tolerance is more often than not another name for indifference; it is mere laziness, lack of interest, a mental shrug of the shoulders. But with Mr. Lynd, tolerance is a passion. Perhaps he discovered it long ago, shining like a rich jewel, in a place where it is all too rarely found, in the country of his birth. Certainly he did discover it, and crossed from Northern Ireland, the home of intolerance, to easy-going England, to preach good-humour. There is nothing strange in this; probably it is only the dusty Arab who can become eloquent in praise of water. We needed some one to whom tolerance was a passion and not a mere habit of mind, to whom it was something hardly earned, in itself a rich reward, so that we could see it anew and realize its worth. No one has helped us to do this more than Mr. Lynd, who has constituted himself the battle champion of good-humour and never becomes angry save on behalf of good temper. "The world is crying out just now for a return of good-humour," he tells us at the beginning of an essay (in *The Passion of Labour*) on the subject; and he praises London, as well he might, for its easy temper: "Lacking its good-humour," he writes, "it would be one of the most uninhabitable of cities. Who would live amid the buzz of eight million spites ? " He follows this up with one of those passages that make this volume such a pleasant little feast of sweet reason :

We too easily forget that good-humour is, after all, the crown and the most lasting of the virtues. There are no great vices save those which are the enemies of good-humour, such as cruelty, meanness, and all forms of crabbed egoism. It is arguable, indeed, that when the great teachers of the world speak of " love " and " charity," they mean for the most part good-humour or good-nature. When we are told to love our enemies we regard it as an impracticable paradox, because we know that no man can love an enemy in the same sense in which he loves his children. It ought to be possible, however, even in one's relations with an enemy, never entirely to lose hold of good-nature. History will record with delight ten thousand instances of good-nature between enemies in the recent war, but of the still more numerous instances of ill-nature we can expect nothing better than a pleasureless palliation. When Paul the Apostle praised charity as the greatest of the virtues, he was but praising good-nature in its highest form.

His essays on criticism so far as they are a plea for anything are a plea for tolerance, and his own critical practice cannot be impeached. It is only intolerance itself that is too much for his forbearance, and only harsh or superior persons, critics with a knout in their hands, excite his anger.

Two things must be remembered in connection with this passion of his for tolerance. The first is that it does not proceed from mere indifference, an absence of convictions. Mr. Lynd has his opinions, democratic and nationalist, and does not hesitate to express them ; indeed, not only has he been an ardent propagandist, but at no time does he really lay his opinions on one side as some essayists do ; and for all its light whimsical air, its gentle high spirits, its occasional excursions into paradox, his work is thoroughly saturated with his general views of life ; and whether he is writing about an author or an egg, there are present in his writing those ethical implications, those indirect references to conduct, that are the mark of a masculine mind in letters. The titles of two of his earlier books (*Home Life in Ireland* and *Rambles in Ireland*) suggest that they formed part of a series designed to assist the prospective tourist, a series of pleasant jog-trot surveys of scenery, history, and manners ; but the curious reader will find that whereas Mr. Lynd gives him some very readable sketches of Irish history, some shrewd observations upon the social life of the country, and (it goes without saying) some amazingly good portraits of Irish character, he has also left out all the topography and scenery and put in all the politics in their place, to the probable confusion of the publisher and his friend, the prospective tourist. Two of his later volumes (*The Passion of Labour* and *If The Germans Conquered England*) are entirely made up of essays on political and social questions, and though they touch upon topical themes for the most part, they are so engagingly written, move so lightly and yet with such sureness, are so seldom flawed with the passion of the moment and reach out to such large issues, that they may be read with delight by the open-minded from now until the next barbarian

invasion. This branch of his work, journalistic in
that it takes up the glove as soon as it is flung down,
philosophical in that it refers the matter to something
beyond the needs of the moment, must be remembered when we come to his more literary and general
essays, for these large interests give his work a background, a standard of reference, without which even
his lightest paper would not be the thing it is. Had he
not written so well on Ruthlessness, Nationality, or
the Importance of Forgetting History, he would not
have written so well on the Betting Man, the Chocolate
Bus, or Riding on a Charabanc. So, too, his criticism
has a biographical trend ; he has a sharper eye for
a man than he has for a book ; he does not linger
over the methods of the art, does not stop to analyse,
but makes straight for his author, and splashes about
in a glittering stream of epigram until he has found the
witty, illuminating phrase : " Horace Walpole was a
dainty rogue in porcelain who walked badly " ; " Oscar
Wilde is a writer whom one must see through in order
to appreciate " ; " Mr. Bennett is at once a connoisseur and a card " ; " Henley was master of the
vainglorious phrase. He was Pistol with a style " ;
and so on. The style of his critical essays—nervous,
pointed, epigrammatic—exactly fits his method ; it
is not a style in which to tell the exact truth, to
suggest the fine shades, but for a lightning portrait,
made up of a few vivid strokes, it can hardly be
excelled, and such portraits are Mr. Lynd's business
in criticism. For the rest, though he is not always
right in his estimates and can grind his little personal

axes with the next critic, he is never dull, always persuasive (sometimes dangerously so), always sane, humorous, tolerant, a man to walk with among books and authors.

The second thing to remember is that this knight-errant of tolerance is an Irishman. Had he been an Englishman, at least a normal Englishman, so optimistic a strain, such an enthusiasm for good-humour, would have left him a very wishy-washy, Skimpole-like creature. Who does not know and contemn the Englishman who has made the national virtue into a vice, who is for ever saying that every opinion is partly true and that there is something to be said for everybody, who brings gruel to the feast of thought? But Mr. Lynd belongs to a race that is mentally harder than the English, more given to sardonic humours, to wit and irony, nearer to black melancholy by many a league; and this smiling enthusiasm of his, instead of making him the author of bright and shallow prattlings, simply acts as a kindly leaven. The result is a full man, that wise, witty, and lovable personality so familiar to readers of *The Pleasures of Ignorance* and *Solomon In All His Glory* and *The Blue Lion*. It is a blend that has made him that very rare person in life and literature—a tolerant and kindly wit, an epigrammatist with a heart.

Some critics and reviewers, in search of a grievance, are always grumbling because our essayists collect their contributions to the Press and make books of them. They seem to imagine that this is yet another sign of the degenerate times, and clearly forget that our best essays have always had their roots in the Press, that our essayists were not called periodical writers for nothing ; and in short, they seem to remember Sir Arthur Helps, and contrive to forget Steele, Addison, Johnson, Goldsmith, Lamb, Hazlitt, Leigh Hunt. They forget that a thing may be both good fun to-day and good literature to-morrow, and that even editors may entertain angels unawares. An essayist may come to the market-place for an hour or so every week, and yet so contrive his utterance that he will afterwards find his way, like the poets, into the library and stay there for ever, blossoming in purple and red. Mr. Lynd's general essays, and particularly those in the three volumes mentioned above, are his most valuable and personal contributions to our literature ; and they only appear in periodicals as men put up for a night at an inn ; their home is in these delightful little volumes, volumes that Mr. Lynd had in his mind all the time he was writing the various papers that compose them. The very fact that these papers have, as it were, successfully buttonholed the casual reader of a periodical is in their favour as pieces of literature ; they grapple with the life about them ; they are true to the kindred points of Heaven and Home ; they begin anywhere, in the street, the house, the fields, and end everywhere ; they take a topic of the moment, an object, a common experience, and relate them to the author's whole vision of life ; they show us the Chocolate Bus in its proper place in the solar system, and relate the betting man to the Milky Way ; they occupy a middle place between poetry and philosophy, but come to us in a homelier guise than either and demand no solemn service of music before they can perform their offices. The author of such papers is a public bene-factor, for he enriches and deepens life, hands on something of his capacity for enjoyment, shames us out of our gloomy indifference by his superior wit and power of observation, and makes us eager to appreciate the significance of little things : we leave his company happier and wiser men. It is true that some of these essays have not that organic nature which makes the true essay as valid a literary form as the lyric or the drama. Every now and then, Mr. Lynd yields to temptation and simply decorates a number of facts with wit and fancy, and so leaves us with the feeling that we have just attended a very bright conjuring trick and not the revelation of a personality. It is a temptation that presses heavily upon an unusually eloquent and ready writer who has his hands full of work, and it is to Mr. Lynd's credit that he does not succumb to it very often.

His greatest asset is his manner, partly natural but probably brought nearer to perfection by great labour, a manner that enables him to take in the most varied matter and to deal with it in a score of different ways, to be whimsical, grave, ironical, humorous in turn, without disturbing his even flow, without that awkward jumping from posture to posture that irritates us in some other, less fortunate, writers. It gives him a freedom in his choice of subjects that is denied to some other essayists who, possessing a less flexible

manner and knowing that their work must be in one
" key," have to restrict themselves very severely in
their choice of subjects and in their attitude towards
those subjects. Mr. Lynd can pass from one theme
to another, very different, theme, from one mood
to another mood, lightly and easily, without a break
in the continuity of his work, like a man idly flashing
on his finger an iridescent jewel. It is this that gives
his essays the quality of exquisitely contrived talk :
a multitude of topics, birds, sportsmen, houses, eggs,
free-lovers, books, insects, the seasons, death and
eternity, come and go, but the voice falling upon our
ears is always the same. He may, for example, write
an essay on Eggs, and make such a confession, a delightful shred or two of gossamer, as this :

I have always thought it one of the chief miseries of being
a man that, when boiled eggs are put on the table, one does not
get first choice, and that all the little brown eggs are taken by
women and children before one's own turn comes round.
There is one sort of egg with a beautiful sunburnt look that
always reminds me of the seaside, and that I have not tasted
in a private house for above twenty years. To begin the day
with such an egg would put one in a good temper for a couple
of hours. But always one is fobbed off with a large white
egg of demonstrative uncomeliness. It may taste all right,
but it does not look all right. Food should appeal to the eye
as well as to the palate, as every one recognizes when the blanc-
mange that has not set is brought to the table.

He may choose to write about *The Shy Fathers* (an
essay that Steele and Lamb would have clapped their
hands over, and one that should go forthwith into
every anthology of modern essays), and describe,

K

in his own lovable fashion, a play performed by children :

To see a play performed by small children with a few foot-lights arranged on the floor in imitation of a theatre, is to feel that all that the saints have said about children is true. How exquisite are their voices, that are all music without the harshness of experience ! To listen to them is like listening to the first birds. To see them is to be back in a world of apple trees in flower. There is comedy in the contrast between them and the grave parts they play and the grave speeches they utter as abbesses, poets, and harpers. But the very mimicry of our grown-up world, which begins by moving us, ends by filling us with bitter-sweet regret that the lives of men and women, after all, are not enacted in voices so sweet and by creatures so fair as these. The feeling may not be a deep one, and may be only for the moment ; but, for the time at least, we wish with a pang that life could always have remained like this, that nobody would ever grow up or die, but that the very kings and admirals and prime ministers and thieves and shopkeepers were all children. It may be that, from the point of view of those who have passed into further æons of existence, kings and admirals and prime ministers and thieves and shopkeepers are so. Who knows but that, in immortal eyes, a conqueror marching from ruined kingdom to ruined kingdom may be but a small boy with a toy sword at his side ? . . .

He may blithely discuss the pleasures of dining, in an essay " On Feeling Gay " :

Marriage, the return of a conquering hero, the visit of a great statesman, the birth of Christ—we find in all these things a reason for calling on the cooks to do their damnedest. Even the dyspeptic forgets his doctor's orders in the general excitement and chases oysters down the narrow stairway of his throat with thick soup, follows thick soup with lobster, and lobster with turkey, and turkey with a savoury, and the savoury with a *pêche Melba*, and at the end of it will not reject cheese and a banana, all of this accompanied with streams of liquid in the form of wine, coffee and brandy. I have often wondered why a man should feel gay doing violence to his entrails in this fashion. I have noticed again and again that he loses a little of his gaiety if the dinner is served slowly enough to give him time to think. The gay meal, like the farce, must be enacted quickly. The very spectacle of waiters hurrying to and fro with an air of peril to the dishes quickens the fancy, and the gastric juices flow to an anapæstic measure. Who does not know what it is to sit through a slow meal and digest in spondees? One is given time between the courses to turn philosopher—to meditate becoming a hermit and dining on a bowl of rice in a cave.

He may write an essay on June, an opulent, coloured thing, and fill it with such eloquent passages as these :

There is no getting beyond the old image of things in general as a stream that disappears. The flowers and the birds come in tides that sweep over the world and in a moment are like a broken wave. The lilacs filled with purple ; laburnum followed, and in a few days all the gold ebbed, and nothing was left but a drift of withered blossoms on the ground ; then came the acacia-flowers, white as the morning among the cool green plumage of the tree, and now they, too, have been turned into dirtiness and deserted foam. And in the hedges change has been as swift, as merciless—change so imperceptible in what it is doing, so manifest in what it has done. The white blossoms of the sloe gave place to the foam of the hawthorn and the flat clusters of the wayfaring tree ; now in its turn has come the flood of the elder-flowers, a flood of commonness, and June on the roads would hardly be beautiful were it not for the roses that settle, delicate and fleeting as butterflies, on the long and crooked briers. . . .

But whatever his theme or his mood, he makes us feel that we are in contact with the same delightful personality, and there is no question here, as there is so often, of our having to cope with half a dozen only partly realized and conflicting personalities. And this is to possess a manner that is indeed enviable.

Like most good essayists, Mr. Lynd, being a homely mediator between philosophy and poetry, can always be discovered generalizing with the philosopher and " particularizing " with the poet. Here, for example, is a comparatively simple passage that concludes his essay on " The Student " :

> The man who has had a University education believes it is the only education worth having. The man who is self-educated believes in self-education as the secret of success. The man who idled at college explains what a blessing his idleness has been to him. The man who has read his eyes out praises God for his labours. Thus, when we look back, we all turn out to have been model students. . . . At the same time, if one had it all to do over again, how eagerly one would consult the pages of Professor Adams for good advice ! How one would plunge into an enthusiasm for work ! And—how one would find oneself the next morning far from the droning lecture-room, smoking a pipe of Navy Cut and discussing the immortality of the soul under the blackening elms of the Botanic Gardens !

And it is worth remarking how the very effective final sentence gains by giving us the particular instances—the " pipe of Navy Cut," the " immortality of the soul," the " blackening elms of the Botanic Gardens." Rewrite the sentence, omitting these concrete illustrations and putting in their place the vague and general statements that most of us would be content to make, and how much is lost. Such writing, a kind of poetry that has a gentle and philosophical gaiety instead of

passion, a poetry in pipe and slippers, knows the value
of imagery, and feeds the imagination as well as the
intellect.   When a man is the master of such a style
and has unusual powers of observation, a notable
sense of humour, and a magnificent capacity for
enjoyment, there is no gainsaying him : he has us
in thrall.   He can bring anything into literature,
even Lyons' tea-shops :

> Their white-and-gold faces and their polished windows
> are as noticeable as the painted signs of inns.   They have a
> nice suggestion that luxury has been democratized and brought
> within the reach of anybody who has threepence in his pocket.
> They announce entertainment.   They seem to say that there
> is no need to go to White Cities in order to be happy while
> toasted scones may be eaten within from marble tables.
> Could Sardanapalus himself ask for anything better than to
> be allowed to sit at a marble table and eat steak-and-kidney
> pudding from a silver fork ?   It is no wonder that Londoners
> flock every day in thousands into these white palaces of poached
> eggs on toast.

Or even the betting man, whose portrait Mr. Lynd
has painted so faithfully that it need never be painted
again :

> Perhaps, in the train on the way home from the races, he
> may relax a little.   Certainly, if he has backed Cutandrum,
> he will.   For Cutandrum won at ten to one, and his pocket is
> full of five-pound notes.   He feels quite jocular now that the
> strain is over.   He makes puns on the names of the defeated
> horses.   " Lie Low lay low all right," he announces to the
> compartment, indifferent to the scowls of the man in the
> corner who had backed it.   " Hopscotch didn't hop quite fast
> enough."   Were he tipsy, he could not jest more fluently.
> His jokes are small, but be not too severe on him.   The man
> has had a hard day.   Wait but an hour, and care will descend

on him again. He will not have sat down to dinner in his hotel for three minutes till some one will be saying to him: " Have you heard anything for the Cup to-morrow ? " There is no six-hours day for the betting man. He is the drudge of chance for every waking hour.

But good as he is on such subjects, he is even better when he forsakes the town for the country. Writing as one ignorant of the subject, the present writer cannot say whether Mr. Lynd's delightful essays about birds add anything to natural history, but they certainly help to shift the balance of pleasure and pain in human history. Birds innumerable flutter through these essays, and always his style lifts and takes wing to follow them. One of his books opens and closes on the subject of birds; it begins with a kingfisher, so prettily, so cunningly :

Not to have seen a kingfisher leaves the world full of a mysterious beauty. There is still something to be sought for— something prettier than the North Pole, before it was dis- covered, and less impossible as an object of search than the Holy Grail. Every river bank along which one wanders is rich with its unseen colours. Not a willow grows aslant a brook but might be the perch of this winged rainbow . . .

and it closes with an essay on Wild Life in London that ends in this fashion :

It is better to be content to say, as anyone may say, " I have seen rooks in Rotten Row. I have seen bats over the Serpentine." For even these things, common though they are, never cease to delight. The rook, the bat and the sea- gull—how a dead city breaks into life at a mere movement of their wings !

And he is never so full of grace and charm as he is when he is writing about these delicate creatures. There are a hundred and one passages as excellent in every way as the following, and yet how good it is :

The wren, brown as a withering leaf, pauses and reattempts the ancient vehemence of its song as it hops among the lower branches of the confused hedge of thorn, sloe and bramble. But for the most part it is content to chatter—to scold no one in particular with its grating churr but the universe or the young moon. The robins are more generous, and recognize that there are other themes for song than love. That, I think, is what has endeared the robin to man. Most of the other birds are amorists in their music. The robins declare that life is good even after the honeymoon, and that there are twelve months in the year, all of them good. They are birds with all the human vices—greedy, quarrelsome and domineering—but at least they sing songs of experience that echo our own—songs in which joy and sorrow, memory and hope, are intermingled beyond extrication.

Or (to give way to temptation yet once again) this passage, in which he writes of those who live so much in their memories :

Even we, however, are sensualists of the open air, and the spectacle of the wind foaming among the leaves of the oak and elm can easily make us forget all but the present. The blue hills in the distance when rain is about, the grey arras of wet that advances over the plain, the whitethroat that sings or rather scolds above the hedge as he dances on the wing, the tree-pipit—or is it another bird ?—that sinks down to the juniper-tip through a honey of music, a rough sea seen in the distance, half-shine, half-scowl—any of these things may easily cut us off from history and from hope and immure us in the present hour.

The style of these essays demands a last word. Those readers who send their eyes, but not their ears, to keep appointments with books will probably underestimate this prose. It has been designed in the first place for the narrow columns of a periodical and so has been broken up into short sentences, simply for the benefit of the eye ; but unlike the style of his critical papers it is not really a short-sentence style at all. Compare it with true " snip-snap " that takes a breath every other moment, avoids conjunctions, and achieves a mechanical, rattling effect, coming to the ear like the noise of a machine-gun, and the difference is plain. Mr. Lynd's prose has variety, modulation ; like all good prose, it has a rhythm of its own. Occasionally it descends into " snip-snap," but generally, beneath its quiet ease and gentle " hurry of the spirit," there is some very delicate modulation, and a certain characteristic rhythm, present even in his earliest essays in *Irish and English*, that turns this prose into a voice. But what has happened is that Mr. Lynd has punctuated for the eye rather than for the ear ; and if space allowed it would be interesting to re-punctuate and regroup one or two characteristic passages. Many of his full-stops are not recognized by the ear as full-stops, but as semicolons and colons ; the rhythm flows on from sentence to sentence, and what appear breaks to the eye (between one sentence and another) are not proper pauses to the ear, busy with the melody. This is not to assert that Mr. Lynd punctuates wrongly, for apart from logical and grammatical considerations, punctuation is simply a system of notation for the ear, and therefore a matter for individual taste. But it may be doubted whether Mr. Lynd has not lost some readers' ears while he has been catching their eyes, and it is the ear alone that can appreciate the felicities of such excellent prose. This, however, is no great matter, and it is probably the only one in which Admetus has robbed Apollo in Mr. Lynd's work; for he has served both these masters, as one of them served the other, and he has served them faithfully and well, as few men in our time have done. Such a writer, with no thin, undersized talent to be nourished on the Virol of sympathy and seclusion, would not have been the magnificent proseman he is, had it not been for the circumstance that made him create literature out of what lay about him, out of his day's work. He is one of the ambassadors from this generation who will recount the homelier affairs of our time to Prince Posterity.

MR. GEORGE SAINTSBURY

WHEN Mr. Saintsbury remarks in Hazlitt's criticism " the *gusto*, the spirit, the inspiriting quality " . . . " that amorous quest of literary beauty and rapturous enjoyment of it . . ." he is, I think, saving us the trouble of finding words to describe the essential quality of his own criticism. And though this central flame burns less brightly in the modern critic, the fact of its being there at all is certainly more to be wondered at. For Hazlitt, like some other of our great critics, was a desultory reader, who browsed where he pleased and followed his nose in criticism. It is true that he gave certain courses of lectures—the English Poets, the Comic Writers, the Dramatic Literature of the Age of Queen Elizabeth, which are among the happiest things in English criticism : but they are not literary history. In them Hazlitt does not map the country, but contents himself, and us too, with describing, with his singular felicity, the towering peaks and various great landmarks. That he could do this with such astonishing sureness of touch without knowing much or anything of minor persons is proof enough of his critical genius, but it does not give us much cause to wonder at his retaining that enthusiasm which has been remarked in him.

No one who has read widely in critical literature can have failed to notice that the literary historian, who has "to read everything," to devour methodically great masses of literature, to bring order into a bewildering array of names and dates, usually shows us little of this gusto, this "amorous quest of literary beauty." The dead weight of books is usually too much for him. In the end the method remains; there is order where before there was chaos; but alas! the spirit has long since fled, and what we finally receive are the cold judgments of a man who has substituted a formula for a critical palate, a day's duty for a delicate but insatiable appetite. This in part explains why there has been such a gulf between our great critics, supremely felicitous in judgment, and our literary historians. Of the latter it would be foolish to speak slightingly, for they have done some wonderful pioneer work; but how many have given us the things, perhaps only phrases, that are keys to new treasure-chambers of literature?

Now, the great, and perhaps peculiar, glory of Professor Saintsbury is that he has retained this gusto, this central flame of literary enthusiasm, throughout a long career (be it noted that he is treated here as a writer) devoted to the chronicling of literary history and similar ventures. Note, first, the sheer bulk of his work: several volumes of essays on individual writers, periods, styles, and what not; anthologies and various editing work; biographies; histories of English, French, European literatures; histories of criticism, English prosody, English prose rhythm ; the novel, English and French ; and so forth. The list is amazing : the mere sight of it intimidates one and makes the more indolent of us wonder what we do with our time. But mere bulk tells us comparatively little. As some ubiquitous contemporaries have shown us, it is not difficult to suggest solid achievement, at least in the catalogues, by dint of hashing and rehashing. I have heard of a certain tradesman, now dead, who had a passion for collecting execrable verse and making books of it, until at last he took up more space in the literary reference books than almost any living writer. But if we examine some of the volumes in this list, and think of what went to the making of them, our wonder and admiration can only grow. To say, as Professor Saintsbury himself does somewhere, that he has " undertaken some tough literary ventures " in his time is only to understate the matter. With the audacity of an Elizabethan sea-captain, he has put out his cockle-boats into vast uncharted oceans of literature, and returned triumphant, laden with glittering spoil and odorous with strange spices.

Consider the three-volume *History of English Prosody*, the *History of English Prose Rhythm*, and, greatest of all, the immense *History of Criticism*, that epic of literary taste. Labours as vast (Courthorpe's *History of English Poetry*, for example) have been successfully accomplished even with us ; Germany and, latterly, America have been prolific of such things and can show us bibliographies of an incredible size. But where else can we find, going along with these things and leavening them, raising them to a higher power, that unflagging spirit which we have already remarked in Professor Saintsbury, that keen savouring of literature, that enthusiasm, with its train of half-humorous and wholly admirable hyperboles, which never deserts him even in his most herculean labours? Throughout he never declines from the critic proper, apt to appreciate and compare, to the mere recorder with his blunted palate and lack-lustre eye. Hardly ever do we meet with the weary gesture, so familiar elsewhere, that directs the author and his work to their appointed pigeon-hole, the particular kind. Notwithstanding the vast scope of his research, the book never becomes to him merely a thing to be classified; it is always a prospective source of delight; and it is in that spirit, the only one for a critic to work in, that we see him approach book after book, writer after writer, in all that great mass of literature through which he has guided us. And it is this almost unique combination of extraordinarily wide reading and research and unflagging appreciation, gusto (call it what you will), that makes him so rare a critic, so delightful a guide and companion in letters, for these and any other times. There is such a brave and human spirit shining through everything that he has written that one is stupefied at the queer epithets —" academic," " pedantic," and the like—that have been hurled at him by novelists turned critics and others; until one remembers that to such persons, he has had the pedantry, the pedagogical insolence, to prefer Shakespeare and Fielding, Thackeray and

Shelley, Dryden and Swift, to them and their friends.

It is easier to say—off-hand—what Professor Saintsbury's critical position is not than what it is. His criticism is known to us as it should be known—by its fruits. But if it is its roots that we wish to disentangle, one or two passages from his *History of Criticism* may be of some service. Replying to those who pronounced him wanting in philosophy in his *History of Criticism*, he wrote :

I hold that the province of Philosophy is occupied by matters of the pure intellect : and that literary criticism is busied with matters which, though not in the loosest meaning, are matters of sense. I do not know—and I do not believe that anyone knows, however much he may juggle with terms —why certain words arranged in certain order stir one like the face of the sea, or like the face of a girl, while other arrangements leave one absolutely indifferent or excite boredom or dislike. I know that we may generalize a little ; may " push our ignorance a little farther back " ; may discover some accordances of sound, some rhythmical adjustments, some cunning and more or less constant appeals to eye and ear which, as we coolly say, " explain " emotion and attraction to some extent. But *why* these general things delight man he knows no more than, in his own more unsophisticated stage, why their individual cases and instances do so. I do not think that my own doctrine of the Poetic (or the literary) Moment —of the instant and mirific " kiss of the spouse "—is so utterly " unphilosophical " : but I do know that that doctrine, if it does not exactly laugh to scorn theories of æsthetic, makes them merely facultative indulgences. And just as physiology, and biology, and all the 'ologies that ever were 'ologied, leave you utterly uninformed as to the real reason of the rapture of the physical kiss, so I think that æsthetics do not teach the reason of the amorous peace of the Poetic Moment.

As a pendant to this, particularly to the " matters of sense " part of it, we may add an earlier passage from the Tennyson essay in *Corrected Impressions :*

Readers, and I hope they are many, of Maginn's *Story without a Tail* will remember the various reasons assigned for taking a dram, until the candid narrator avowed that he took it " because he liked a dram." It is undoubtedly natural to humanity to disguise to itself the reasons and nature of its enjoyments ; but I do not know that it exhibits this possibly amiable and certainly amusing weakness more curiously or more distinctly in any matter than in the matter of poetry. Men will try to persuade themselves, or at least others, that they read poetry because it is a criticism of life, because it expresses the doubts and fears and thoughts and hopes of the time, because it is a substitute for religion, because it is a relief from serious work, because and because and because. As a matter of fact, they (that is to say, those of them who like it genuinely) read it because they like it, because it communicates an experience of half-sensual, half-intellectual pleasure to them. *Why* it does this no mortal can say, any more than he can say why the other causes of his pleasures produce their effect. *How* it does, it is perhaps not quite so hard to explain ; though here also we come as usual to the bounding-wall of mystery before very long. And it is further curious to note that the same kind of prudery and want of frankness comes in here once more. It often makes people positively angry to be told that the greatest part, if not the whole, of the pleasure-giving appeal of poetry lies in its sound rather than its sense, or, to speak with extreme exactness, lies in the manner in which the sound conveys the sense. No " chain of extremely valuable thoughts " is poetry in itself : it only becomes poetry when it is conveyed with those charms of language, metre, rhyme, cadence, what not, which certain persons disdain.

Here we have the doctrine of literature for our good pleasure's sake, of omnific form and its peculiar emotion, stated with a vengeance. Innumerable idols are tumbled down that the Word itself, mysterious, imperishable, may be throned on high. And throned with it, or above it, is the omnicompetent and omnipotent personal taste, from whose judgment there is no appeal. Some there may be who doubt whether actual practice in criticism can go very far on the lines we have seen laid down. If so, let them read in Professor Saintsbury's unnumbered volumes and decide for themselves. But they must not, of course, expect that cast-iron consistency from which our best English critics—happily, I think—have always been free. I can at least save such doubters and scoffers some trouble by taking them straight to a very promising little battleground, cleared and ready for the drums and tramplings of critical battalions ; it is a passage from his *History of Nineteenth Century Literature*, and it runs as follows :

But the Ode (Wordsworth's *Intimations of Immortality*) remains not merely the greatest, but the one really dazzlingly, supremely great thing he ever did. Its theory has been scorned or impugned by some ; parts of it have been called nonsense by critics of weight. But, sound or unsound, sense or nonsense, it is poetry, and magnificent poetry, from the first line to the last—poetry than which there is none better in any language, poetry such as there is not perhaps more than a small volume-full in all languages.

It is not, of course, the judgment itself that will sound the trumpet-call to arms, but the cool " Sense or Nonsense—this is great poetry ! "

Turning again to the *History of Criticism*, we may note, with approval, disgust, or mere amusement, a very characteristic passage expressing the critic's distrust of the definition :

> The port was the Fair Haven of Romanticism, and the purpose was to distinguish " that which is established because it is right from that which is right because it is established," as Johnson himself formulates it. And now, of course, the horse-leeches of definition will ask me to define Romanticism, and now, also, I shall do nothing of the sort, and borrow from the unimpeachable authority of M. Brunetière (*quoted in note*) my reason for not doing it. What most of the personages of this book sought or helped (sometimes without at all seeking) to establish is Romanticism, and Romanticism is what they sought or helped to establish. In negative and by contrast, as usual, there is, however, no difficulty in arriving at a sort of jury-definition, which is perhaps a good deal better to work to port with than the aspiring but rather untrustworthy mast-poles of " Renascence of Wonder " and the like. We have indeed seen, throughout the last volume, that the curse and the mischief of Neo-classicism lay in the tyranny of the Definition itself. You had no sooner satisfied yourself that Poetry was such and such a thing, that it consisted of such and such narrowly delimited Kinds, that its stamped instruments and sealed patterns were this and that, than you proceeded to apply these propositions inquisitorially, excommunicating or executing delinquents and nonconformists.

A further danger of the definition in criticism, a danger from which Professor Saintsbury has naturally been free, but one that has ensnared not a few critics of the last century, is that it tends to push the actual work into the background and itself into the foreground. Thus a body of work is given, perhaps for the sake of mere convenience, a certain label— romantic, neo-classical, realistic, naturalistic, or the like. Before long the " horse-leeches " are attracted by the label, and one or more definitions are fastened

L

to it. From now on critics begin to batten on the definitions or quarrel about them and, all the while, the work itself, the only real thing and the only thing that matters, is fading further and further into the background. The ordinary reader begins to peer through the spectacles of definition, and risks losing whole periods of literature that would normally have proved a delight to him.

Another danger, one that is not so pressing now, though still liable to threaten from unexpected quarters, and one against which Professor Saintsbury has ever been careful to guard himself, is the critical fallacy of " This is beautiful but not to be tolerated." There is a characteristic explosion against this doctrine of monstrous beauty in the *History of English Prose Rhythm*, which may be quoted as an example of many things. It follows the quotation of a very beautiful passage in Ruskin's most opulent and puissant style :

Now, of course, it obviously may be said, and probably has been said a hundred times, that this is illegitimate, a "monstrous beauty," something that " you *ought not* to like." Well, this is the seventh vial-volume (I blush for it) that I have opened in hope of pouring contempt and destruction on the doctrine of monstrous beauties. It is impossible that beauty should be monstrous ; and if I met a monster that pretended to be one and was beautiful, I should, like Prince Seithenyn, tell it to its beautiful face that it was no monster. But *is* this beautiful ? There of course we come to the old flaming walls of the world of taste. I can only say that if it is not, I do not know where beauty of prose is to be found.

As yet, however, we have seen more of the negative than the positive side of his theory and practice.

But there is a passage in the conclusion of the *History of Criticism,* the result perhaps of the expansive mood that often comes at the end of a long labour, in which he proclaims the critical faith that is in him :

But it may fairly be asked, How do you propose to define *any* principles for your New Critic ? And the answers are ready, one in Hellenic, one in Hebraic phraseology. The definition shall be couched as the man of understanding would define it : and if any will do the works of the New Criticism he shall know the doctrine thereof. Nor are the works themselves hard to set forth. He must read, and, as far as possible, read everything—that is the first and great commandment. If he omits one period of a literature, even one author of some real, if ever so little, importance in a period, he runs the risk of putting his view of the rest out of focus ; if he fails to take at least some account of other literatures as well, his state will be nearly as perilous. Secondly, he must constantly compare books, authors, literatures indeed, to see in what each differs from each, but never in order to dislike one because it is not the other. Thirdly, he must, as far as he possibly can, divest himself of any idea of what a book *ought to be*, until he has seen what it is. In other words, and to revert to the old simile, the plate to which he exposes the object cannot be too carefully prepared and sensitised, so that it may take the exactest possible reflection : but it cannot also be too carefully protected from even the minutest line, shadow, dot, that may affect or predetermine the impression in the very slightest degree.

Now, it is not so much his critical theory as his practice that we are concerned with here. With any born critic, I maintain, the two are never quite the same : his practice is always wider, deeper, more embracing than his theory. There is certainly nothing that Professor Saintsbury lays down above that he has not put into his own practice. No one can deny the scope of his reading, and few can be blind to his extensive use of the comparative method. This last is, I think, the source of one of his weaknesses, one chiefly to be found in his histories of special periods, where it may be partly excused by the lack of space. The weakness in question is a tendency to emphasize the continuity and development of the literature itself at the expense of the individual writers who compose that literature ; a habit of explaining everybody in terms of everybody else, so that while one learns that B. (that great genius) is better than A., who paved the way for him, but not so wonderful as C., who followed after, one still feels uncomfortably ignorant about B. But when this is said, it is only fair to add that the literary historians on the other side, the " Forces," " Tendencies," " Spirit of the Time " mongers, are as a rule infinitely more unjust to their individual authors. Still there must be a good many of Professor Saintsbury's readers (and those not the least enthusiastic) who have been impressed by a certain lack of finality about his treatment of individual writers. This is in part also due to what appears to be his dislike of pushing an analysis very far. Often he leaves the lemon before he has squeezed it dry ; after indicating a few well-marked characteristics, he is apt to take refuge too quickly in one of the innumerable terms, beginning, say, at the " je ne sais quoi " and ending somewhere near that mysterious verb " fondoos," he uses to describe the mystery of personality and genius. But if the method has sometimes left him weak where a few—a very few—other critics are strong, it has also made his stronghold of taste, comparison, and estimate impregnable when so many critical fortresses have been tumbling about their captains' ears. It has given him a sureness of touch in handling large masses of literature, the history of whole periods or special kinds, that is the admiration of students and the despair of critics who follow in his wake. Further, combined with certain innate qualities of mind, it has made him the best critic of critics, the best historian of books about books, in our literature. The humorless and timid academic may be alienated by certain peculiar—but, I think, delightful—idiosyncrasies of style and manner ; other persons, who have axes to grind and are secretly afraid of his wide reading and hatred of fashionable literary cant, may pretend a great disdain ; but those readers who have followed in his tracks find themselves turning again and again to his innumerable felicitous judgments with ever-increasing admiration and gratitude.

He has, of course, his limitations, most of them the natural limitations for which experienced readers are able to allow. I for one do not think that he shows the same extraordinary sureness of touch in dealing with literature produced, say, since 1850 that he does in dealing with work of an earlier date : it is not to be expected. He always shows, too, a tendency to react overmuch against current enthusiasms, against writers whom it is the fashion to praise. This, however, is not very deplorable, nor very unnatural; it comes from the desire, deep-seated in every true critic, to adjust the balance, to throw some weight into the lighter scale. Thus, when every one is clustered about the swings, Professor Saintsbury does not hesitate to come forward and praise the exquisite and delectable roundabouts. He has, as his readers know, some strong opinions and his fair share of rather Peacockian crotchets. He professes a creed of Toryism so extreme, so fantastic, that it probably has no fellow in these islands. He can take a strongly partisan interest in our politics up to 1832, but after that it is simply a matter of our going to the dogs at varying rates of speed. For the rest, he can still call Cambridge " the Whig University," and he may, for all I know to the contrary, be the last of the Jacobites. His attitude is so astonishing and puts him, for most of us at least, so far beyond the pale of controversy that one could no more quarrel with him about it than one could with Peacock's delightful Doctor Folliott, with whom he has much in common. Anyone who wishes to see the crotchets bristling has only to turn to his invaluable *Peace of the Augustans*, and in particular to a passage on Johnson. But even in this volume, where he makes very unfair though entertaining comparisons between an eighteenth century that he clearly understands and loves and a twentieth century that he plainly does not care to understand and love—even here he performs his task supremely well; it is his business to comment upon the literature of the older century, and this he does magnificently. Crotchets or no crotchets, not once does he play the traitor to his love of letters ; not once does he deny the Muse and conceal his delight or find none, because of extra-literary considerations. On the other hand, there are not a few writers whose characters are the very ones with which he is least likely to have any sympathy, whose views and aims must be abhorrent to him, to whom he has been one of the first to do full justice. No one, for example, has given Shelley a higher place among our poets. And no one has recognized more justly and generously the amazing critical genius of Coleridge, who has been so seriously underestimated by more than one critic of our time.

Again, no one has been bolder in speaking out when such a thing has been necessary. We must make no mistake about this. It is easy enough to speak out or to play the part of *l'enfant terrible* in criticism if one has no critical conscience and is a devotee of mere impudence in literary judgment, or addicted to what Professor Saintsbury himself calls the practice of " ragging." But for a critic who knows the English, nay, European tradition of literary judgment, and is himself working in that tradition, it requires no little courage and honesty to speak out against a weight of great authority. There was weight enough on the side of Byron as a great poet when the following passage, one example out of many of " speaking out," was written by Professor Saintsbury nearly thirty years ago. The passage is not quoted, be it understood, as a final estimate of

Byron, for its purpose is simply to show what Byron is *not*:

Byron, then, seems to me a poet distinctly of the second class, and not even of the best kind of second, inasmuch as his greatness is chiefly derived from a sort of parody, a sort of imitation, of the qualities of the first. His verse is to the greatest poetry what melodrama is to tragedy, what plaster is to marble, what pinchbeck is to gold. He is not, indeed, an impostor; for his sense of the beauty of nature and of the unsatisfactoriness of life is real, and his power of conveying this sense to others is real also. He has great, though uncertain, and never very *fine*, command of poetic sound, and a considerable though less command of poetic vision. But in all this there is a singular touch of illusion, of what his contemporaries had learnt from Scott to call gramarye. The often cited parallel of the false and true Florimels in Spenser applies here also. The really great poets do not injure each other in the very least by comparison, different as they are. Milton does not "kill" Wordsworth; Spenser does not injure Shelley; there is no danger in reading Keats immediately after Coleridge. But read Byron in close juxtaposition with any of these, or with not a few others, and the effect, to any good poetic taste, must surely be disastrous; to my own, whether good or bad, it is perfectly fatal. The light is not that which never was on land or sea; it is that which is habitually just in front of the stage: the roses are rouged, the cries of passion even sometimes (not always) ring false. I have read Byron again and again; I have sometimes, by reading Byron only and putting a strong constraint upon myself, got nearly into the mood to enjoy him. But let eye or ear once catch sight or sound of real poetry and the enchantment vanishes.

Here, too, we may notice more fully what has already been touched upon, his hatred of, and onslaughts upon, fashionable literary cant. Nor does he restrict himself to demolishing men of straw, cheap phrases and cheaper attitudes, but fears not to attack things that have passed current in some very good circles ; so that even the great practitioners are not safe from him ; not even Coleridge, as witness his very neat counter (*Hist. Eng. Criticism*, page 333) to Coleridge's famous and over-quoted gibe at the opening couplet of the *Vanity of Human Wishes*. There is a very characteristic onslaught upon one of those phrases that reviewers are too apt to inflict upon their readers in his *History of English Prose Rhythm*, a volume, by the way, that is crammed with perhaps unexpected entertainment :

In touching on the prose of William Morris, it is hardly possible to avoid a small *excursus* of controversy, such as I have elsewhere for the most part eschewed. Critics of worship have pronounced his method " Wardour Street " ; and in Wardour Street, or out of it, there can, it seems, come no good thing. Well, that was pretty much Ben Jonson's objection to Spenser ; and I do not think the best judgment of posterity has endorsed it. For my part, I have no more antecedent objection to thing or person because the street from which it comes is named " Wardour " than I have preference for it because that street is named " Regent " or " Rivoli." All I want to know is whether it is beautiful and delightful. For me, I find beauty and delight in Morris's following of Mandeville and Malory and some saga-men, not only now and then, not only not seldom, but very nearly always. It is, of course, like all falsettos, liable to a breakdown ; and this sometimes, though not very often, occurs. At other times it seems to me extremely agreeable, and very nearly your only style for the matter. If anybody does not want the matter, well and good ; let him leave it alone. I want the matter and I like the style.

Another and not less characteristic passage, attacking an attitude of mind that is now very common and not very healthy, can be culled from his *History of the English Novel.* He is objecting to the not un-natural but *extra*-natural way in which Meredith manages to colour his representation of story and character, and gives instances. He goes on :

They (some of the principal characters) are not impossible : they could be translated into actual tellurian beings, which the men and women of the bad novelist never can be. But at present they are not translated : and you must know a special language, in a wide sense, in order to translate them. I do not say that the language is impossible or even very hard to learn : but it is required. And Meredithians say you ought to learn it. An extremely respectable book of reference before me rebukes " those who lack the intelligence and sensibility that can alone admit them to the charmed circle of appreciative readers " and who " have not patience to apply themselves to the study of the higher fiction with the same ardour that they think necessary in the case of any other art." Now " Fudge ! " is a rude word : but I fear we must borrow it from Goldsmith's hero and apply it here. As for " charmed circles " there is uncommonly good company outside them, where, as Beatrice says, we may " be as merry as the day is long," so that the Comic Spirit cannot entirely disdain us. And as for art—the present writer will fight for its claims as long as he has breath. But the proof of the art of the novelist is that—at first hand or very shortly—he " enfists," absorbs, delights you. You may discover secrets of his art afterwards with much pleasure and profit ; but the actual first-hand delight is the criterion. There ought to be no need of sitting down before the thing with tools and dynamite like burglars at a safe ; of mustering crucibles and reagents like assayers at some doubtful and recalcitrant piece of ore. Now these not very adept defenders of Mr. Meredith seem to assert that these processes are desirable in any case, and necessary in his. As a matter of fact the necessity is not omnipresent : but it is present far too frequently. It is the first duty of the novelist to " let himself be read "—anything else that he gives you is a *bonus*, a trimming, a dessert.

It is possible, nay, probable, that I have been parting company with not a few well-disposed persons all along the route up to this point. I shall probably part company with many more from now onwards, for we have come inevitably to some discussion of Professor Saintsbury's style, that famous style over which so many people, themselves not likely to figure in any anthologies of prose, have made merry. Like most styles that are truly styles and native to their users, it has been largely conditioned by the work it has had to perform. The sort of style that will do admirably for little meditative essays on Love and Death will be little use for the writing of literary histories, in which an immense array of facts and a prodigious number of opinions have to be presented in the smallest possible space. Our prettiest stylists have usually kept clear of such rough-hewing work. In his *History of English Prose Rhythm* Professor Saintsbury is very depreciatory and humorous about his own powers : in the preface he quotes with emphasis Diderot's epigram on Beccaria's " ouvrage sur le style où il n'y a point de style," and in the text there are, for the purpose of comparison, numerous references to " Cluvienus and myself." But elsewhere in the volume, on page 351 to be exact, the curious may find a spirited defence of the neologist and the parenthetic writer against the charges of slovenliness and bad grammar put forward by " half-educated critics " and others. So here are clues, if anyone should be blind and deaf enough to need them. The two most characteristic features of his style are, of course, his extraordinary use of parenthesis, clause within clause like the carven globes in the Oriental toys, and his uncommon use of literary allusion. He quotes widely, of course, but is much more given to allusion, ranging from the stock things of literature to rather obscure college jests, all natural enough in a man soaked in letters and of some humour, and eager to lighten his page and pass on good things, or recall them, to his readers. Of the two well-known dangers of allusion and quotation—first, that of being trite and boring ; second, that of being obscure and teasing—he completely escapes the first to fall a victim to the second. There must be a good many people, of whom I am one, who profess to have read and remembered a little, but to whom more than a few of his allusions are still mysteries. His parenthetic manner is simply the result of a full mind, anxious to leave nothing unsaid on the subject in hand, working with little space at its command. There is, too, to be observed in it an entertaining duality in the writer, so that as we read we hear two persons addressing us. Mr. George Saintsbury, the enthusiastic lover of letters, begins the sentence with a smashing hyperbole, but is immediately checked by Professor Saintsbury, the scholar, who points out some exception, a reservation, or what not ; the enthusiast promptly shakes off his interrupter, and gives a side-cut at those for whom it should be necessary to state such reservations, etc. ; so the scholar immediately hints that there is something to be said for them ; and so it goes on. Style and manner are,

of course, so personal that we can only draw nearer
and nearer to "the old flaming walls of the world
of taste." Doubtless there are many readers who
are only irritated by his repeated side-cuts at "critics
of worship," "persons who shall be nameless," and
the rest ; but in its suggestion of a scholarly pugnacity
dashed with old-fashioned courtesy this polemical
manner of his has always given me, for one, more
than a little delight. I have always found some
entertainment, too, in his habit of not merely saying
that a thing is good or excellent, but of applying to
it a whole host of metaphors drawn from precious
metals and stones and (better) eating and drinking.
Surely a man has a right to let off steam somewhere
in a literary history ! There is much to be said for
the hyperbole, judiciously used, even though Macaulay
has made it so unpopular in most quarters. There
may be persons who really dislike an outburst like the
following when they encounter it in a learned hand-
book ; but I for one cannot join them : "To Dr.
Brandes, Scott is an author 'whom no grown-up
person reads '—a generalization perhaps the rashest,
except Tolstoi's, that 'all prostitutes and madmen
smoke,' which, in the course of a large experience of
books, the present writer has registered." As for his
style in general, although I have found it sometimes
clumsy and altogether unlovely, at others irritating
and positively obscure, nevertheless I hold that there
is much to be said in its favour. It suits the matter
(difficult as that usually is to cope with), and it suits
the man. Because it is not a pastiche of the styles

usually held up for imitation, its good qualities are, I fancy, apt to be overlooked. It is not for nothing that this style belongs to the man who has written so much and so well on English prose style and its rhythm in particular. The quotations I have given are mostly in one " key," and more fully representative of opinion than style; but even in them one can mark a certain felicity of rhythm and cadence, a certain crisp ring that falls easily and pleasantly upon the ear, and, of itself, tends to carry conviction. He has, too, some cunning in the long falling close, in which the pace gradually slackens and phrase after phrase goes ebbing out. And when occasion calls for a change of tone, demands that the loose easy style shall be raised into something more closely knit, more dignified and weighty, it does not call in vain, as many fine passages can testify. One such passage there was, that concluding one on Johnson in *The Peace of the Augustans*, I could have wished to quote, but I have quoted enough : let it remain with its fellows, ready to give the lie to those who have spoken hastily and unjustly. To any reader at all disposed to be friendly, this style of Professor Saintsbury's soon ceases to be a trick of assembling words and becomes the fit expression of a strong and winning personality : it becomes a voice. And it is a voice that lures us into places of enchantment, and tells of things infinitely beguiling, and thus earns for ever our gratitude ; while we, on our part, can but stammer our thanks in some such poor way as this, and so remain for ever fathoms deep in debt.

MR. GEORGE SANTAYANA

ABOUT the time that America discovered in W. H. Hudson "one of the greatest masters of English Prose" and so on and so forth, she lost and we gained for a season a prose stylist who is at least Hudson's equal if not his superior—Mr. George Santayana. Mr. Santayana is a unique figure in modern letters. In the first place, he is a genuine cosmopolitan; born some sixty years ago where there runs one of the narrowest and deepest traditions of nationality, in Spain, he went at an early age where nationality is only in the making, to the United States; the rest may be related in his own words, in one of those complimentary passages of his *Soliloquies in England* in which he repays, with astonishing munificence, like some fairy godmother, any debt of gratitude to those who have made him welcome here :

It was with a premonition of things noble and tender, and yet conventional, that after a term at the University of Berlin I went to spend my first holidays in England. Those were the great free days of my youth. I had lived familiarly in Spain and in the United States; I had had a glimpse of France and of Germany, and French literature had been my daily bread; it had taught me how to think, but had not given me much to think about. I was not mistaken in surmising that in England I should find a *tertium quid*, something soberer and juster than anything I yet knew, and at the same time greener and richer. I felt at once that here was a distinctive society, a way of living fundamentally foreign to me, but deeply attractive. At first all gates seemed shut and bristling with incommunication ; but soon in some embowered corner I found the stile I might climb over, and the ancient right of way. Those peaceful parks, and those minds no less retired, seemed positively to welcome me ; and though I was still divided from them by inevitable partitions, these were in places so thin and yielding, that the separation seemed hardly greater than is requisite for union and sympathy between autonomous minds. Indeed, I was soon satisfied that no climate, no manners, no comrades on earth (where nothing is perfect) could be more congenial to my complexion.

Here, then, is one who spent his childhood in Madrid, who has since learnt and taught at Harvard, gaped for a season at Berlin, lectured at the Sorbonne, and meditated at Oxford ; who has babbled in Spanish, chopped logic in German, read in French, and written in English ; a philosophical and literary League of Nations. The advantages of such a position as citizen of the world are perhaps more easily realized than the disadvantages. But it must not be forgotten that philosophers, like other creatures born of women, arrive in this world at a certain time in a certain place ; they imbibe preferences and prejudices with their mother's milk, and tradition, the tradition of their time and place, plays its part one way or the other, inclining them either to a joyful acceptance or a bitter rebellion. The cosmopolitan, who has sat in all the Opera Houses and eaten all the entrées from Paris to Pekin, brings with him a fine air of freedom and knowledge, and appears to stride unfettered by any national prejudices and vices of mind ; but more often than not he is only a tourist instead of a citizen, and has been called upon to face only the trivial problems of the tourist in place of the graver problems of the citizen ; he has lightly avoided the poisonous berries of national life, but so too he has never been sustained by its ancient and life-giving roots. The settled life of a nation, that which it presents to the eye of a traveller, is not really a show hastily though hopefully put together for the benefit of gaping strangers ; it is the result of a long and arduous battle with circumstance, in which human nature has probably been tried to the full extent of its powers and has taken on strange shapes ; there was more in Ithaca than was ever imagined by the traveller who passed an hour or so with the elderly dozing Ulysses and his Penelope. A certain air of detachment and condescension in Mr. Santayana, the air of one who watches a revolution in a little alien state, is the result of this cosmopolitanism of his, which is also partly responsible, I imagine, for his curious eclecticism, his trick of making the best of half a dozen different philosophical worlds.

In the second place, though Mr. Santayana is a philosopher who has spent half his life teaching the subject, he differs from all contemporary philosophers of any importance in three particulars, the breadth of his interests, the manner of his approach to his subject, and his actual style, three particulars that cannot really be separated. He is read and enjoyed by persons who shudder at the sight of the ugly

M

machinery set up by most contemporary philosophers to grind out their speculations on the ultimate nature of reality. Unless we are prepared for it, we are at once surprised and delighted when we take up a volume of contemporary philosophy, a certain *Scepticism and Animal Faith*, let us say, by a Mr. Santayana, and discover passages of this kind almost on every page :

> We may have such determinate minds that the suggestions of experience always issue there in the same dogmas ; and these orthodox dogmas, perpetually revived by the stimulus of things, may become our dominant or even our sole apprehension of them. We shall really have moved to another level of mental discourse ; we shall be living on ideas. In the gardens of Seville I once heard, coming through the tangle of palms and orange trees, the treble voice of a pupil in the theological seminary, crying to his playmate : "You booby ! of course angels have a more perfect nature than men." With his black and red cassock that child had put on dialectic ; he was playing the game of dogma and dreaming in words, and was insensible to the scent of violets that filled the air. . . .

or find the author, pushing his way forward to an ultimate scepticism, denying the past and future to the sceptic, in this fashion :

> The world present to the sceptic may continue to fade into these opposite abysses, the past and the future ; but having renounced all prejudice and checked all customary faith, he will regard both as painted abysses only, like the opposite exits to the country and to the city on the ancient stage. He will see the masked actors (and he will invent a reason) rushing frantically out on one side and in at the other ; but he knows that the moment they are out of sight the play is over for them ; those outlying regions and those reported events which the messengers narrate so impressively are pure fancy ; and

there is nothing for him but to sit in his seat and lend his
mind to the tragic illusion. . . .

There is here some hint of the poet, and if we read
on and go from book to book, staying longest with the
Soliloquies in England, we shall find more of him, this
poet who can make the quiet style, so often deceptively
quiet, flow everywhere into appropriate, persuasive,
enchanting imagery, who can seemingly think in
imagery and not merely rouge and perfume his
prosaic thought, who can press forward to his conclusions by way of his images, so that they appear to
us the living flesh on the bones of his logical structure
and not, as often, mere brocaded cloths flung over a
lay figure. We open the *Later Soliloquies* and discover
such a passage as this :

There is an obscure rumour that after the fall of Troy
Helen never returned to Sparta, but was spirited away to
Egypt, whilst a mere phantasm resembling her accompanied
her dull husband back to his dull fastness by the pebbly
Eurotas. This turn given to the fable hints darkly at an
unearthly truth. Helen was a phantom always and everywhere ; so long as men fought for her, taking her image, as
it were, for their banner, she presided over a most veritable
and bloody battle ; but when the battle ceased of itself, and
all those heroes that had seen and idolized her were dead,
the cerulean colours of that banner faded from it ; the shreds
of it rotted indistinguishly in the mire, and the hues that
had lent it for a moment its terrible magic fled back into the
ether, where wind and mist, meteors and sunbeams, never
cease to weave them. The passing of Helen was the death of
Greece, but Helen herself is its immortality . . .

or, earlier, come upon him contrasting two faiths most
effectively, though not with complete justice, simply
by contrasting two vivid little pictures :

Protestant faith does not vanish into the sunlight as Catholic faith does, but leaves a shadowy ghost haunting the night of the soul. Faith, in the two cases, was not faith in the same sense ; for the Catholic it was belief in a report or an argument ; for the Protestant it was confidence in an allegiance. When Catholics leave the church they do so by the south door, into the glare of the market-place, where their eye is at once attracted by the wares displayed in the booths, by the flower-stalls with their bright awnings, by the fountain with its baroque Tritons blowing the spray into the air, and the children laughing and playing round it, by the concourse of townspeople and strangers, and by the soldiers, perhaps, marching past ; and if they cast a look back at the church at all, it is only to admire its antique architecture, that crumbling filigree of stone so poetically surviving in its incongruous setting. It is astonishing sometimes with what contempt, with what a complete absence of understanding, unbelievers in Catholic countries look back on their religion. For one cultivated mind that sees in that religion a monument to his racial genius, a heritage of poetry and art almost as precious as the classical heritage, which indeed it incorporated in a hybrid form, there are twenty ignorant radicals who pass it by apologetically, as they might the broken toys or dusty schoolbooks of childhood. . . .

Protestants, on the contrary, leave the church by the north door, into the damp solitude of a green churchyard, amid yews and weeping willows and overgrown mounds and fallen illegible gravestones. They feel a terrible chill ; the few weedy flowers that may struggle through the long grass do not console them ; it was far brighter and warmer and more decent inside. The church—boring as the platitudes and insincerities were which you listened to there for hours—was an edifice, some-thing protective, social and human ; whereas here, in this vague unhomely wilderness, nothing seems to await you but dis-couragement and melancholy. Better the church than the madhouse. . . .

We have a right to transfer the creator of these fabrics of rich and meditative prose from the narrow field of philosophy proper to the wider field of letters.

If Philosophy, a school-marm for ever trying to live down her past indiscretions, has looked somewhat coldly upon Mr. Santayana, Literature, who holds out her arms to her children no matter from what queer place they start up, will give him all the warmer welcome. Philosophy, however, has some excuse for her attitude. An American historian of modern speculative thought begins his notice of our author by remarking that—" George Santayana's lack of influence in proportion to the weight of his contribution to philosophical sanity and clarity, perhaps due in part to the academic distrust of literary gifts, is also not unconnected with a tone of condescension which he is apt to adopt toward competing views, as calling for indulgence rather than for serious argument. In consequence his work is more impressive as an imaginative picture of a certain outlook on the spiritual life of man, than for its explicit dialectical groundling." In an able notice of Mr. Santayana in the *Times Literary Supplement*, an anonymous philosophical critic, after commenting adversely on his author's methods and conclusions, remarked—" To look through the ' Life of Reason ' again after seventeen years is to feel even more strongly than at the original reading how sterile that system must be from which the insight, the sympathy, the imaginative sweep, the richly furnished memory of Mr. Santayana can elicit no better answers to radical questions. In book after book since that

treatise was first published Mr. Santayana has gone
on adding to our best treasures of literary and social
criticism ; but if, as he allows us on the whole to
presume, he still retains his old standpoint in
philosophy, how little he has to offer in that field ! ”
In an essay in the *Soliloquies*, *On My Friendly Critics*,
he discusses, half-playfully, half-earnestly, the various
criticisms that have been passed both upon him and
his work :

As to my person, my critics are very gentle, and I am sensible
of the kindness, or the diffidence, with which they treat me.
I do not mind being occasionally denounced for atheism,
conceit or detachment. One has to be oneself ; and so long
as the facts are not misrepresented—and I have little to complain of on that score—any judgment based upon them is a
two-edged sword : people simply condemn what condemns
them. I can always say to myself that my atheism, like that of
Spinoza, is true piety towards the universe and denies only
gods fashioned by men in their own image, to be servants of
their human interests ; and that even in this denial I am no
rude iconoclast, but full of secret sympathy with the impulses
of idolaters. My detachment from things and persons is also
affectionate, and simply what the ancients called philosophy :
I consent that a flowing river should flow ; I renounce that
which betrays, and cling to that which satisfies, and I relish
the irony of truth ; but my security in my own happiness is
not indifference to that of others ; I rejoice that every one
should have his tastes and his pleasures. That I am conceited,
it would be folly to deny : what artist, what thinker, what
parent does not over-estimate his own offspring ? Can I
suppress an irresistible sense of seeing things clearly, and a
keen delight in so seeing them ?

There is, of course, a good deal that could be said
about the above by those friendly critics, who might
ask, for example, how much affection goes with

detachment and how far something more than indifference to the happiness of others makes for the security of one's own happiness. He then passes on to discuss his impersonal opinions, and though the remainder of the essay is much too long to quote in full, it is worth noticing because it gives us, I think, a better clue to his real position than his more formal statements elsewhere. It is all curiously shifting. He defends his extreme naturalism :

> Any existing persons, and any gods exercising power, will evidently be parts of nature. . . . Every assertion about existence is hazarded, it rests on animal faith, not on logical proof ; and every argument to support naturalism, or to rebut it, implies naturalism. To deny that there are any facts (if scepticism can be carried so far) is still to dogmatize, no less than it would be to point to some fact in particular ; in either case we descend into the arena of existence, which may betray our confidence. Any fact is an existence which discourse plays about and regards, but does not create. . . .

The basis of this naturalism is really science :

> I have no metaphysics, and in that sense I am no philosopher, but a poor ignoramus trusting to what he hears from the men of science. I rely on them to discover gradually exactly which elements in their description of nature may be literally true, and which merely symbolical : even if they were all symbolical, they would be true enough for me. . . .

But on this thoroughgoing naturalism is magically erected a kind of picturesque Platonism that is a dream without even a dreamer ; values flower out of nothing ; if, as Mr. Santayana declares :

> I am quite happy in this human ignorance mitigated by pictures, for it yields practical security and poetic beauty :

what more can a sane man want ? In this respect I think sometimes I am the only philosopher living : I am resigned to being a mind . . .

he seems like a mind in mid-air. Later, he remarks that " men of the world, when they dip into my books, find them consistent, almost oppressively con- sistent, and to the ladies everything is crystal-clear " ; it is only the philosophers who misunderstand. This is probably true, but what the men of the world and the ladies find consistent and crystal-clear is the writer's temperament and his manner of expressing that temperament ; the philosophers are in search of convictions and discover that Mr. Santayana's are for ever eluding their grasp. After further discussing a tendency of his to take up various philosophical positions that were, however, nothing more to him than " theoretic poses or possibilities ; vistas for the imagination, never convictions," merely waking dreams to be entered into even yet at will ; he comes to a point that is of particular interest :

In moral philosophy (which is my chosen subject) I find my unsophisticated readers, as I found my pupils formerly, delightfully appreciative, warmly sympathetic, and altogether friends of mine in the spirit. It is a joy, like that of true con- versation, to look and laugh and cry at the world so unfeignedly together. But the other philosophers, and those whose religion is of the anxious and intolerant sort, are not at all pleased. They think my morality very loose : I am a friend of publicans and sinners, not (as they are) in zeal to reform them, but because I like them as they are ; and indeed I am a pagan and a moral sceptic in my naturalism. On the other hand (and this seems a contradiction to them), my moral philosophy looks strangely negative and narrow ; a philosophy of abstention and distaste for life. What a horrible combination, they say to themselves, of moral licence with moral poverty ! They do not see that it is because I love life that I wish to keep it sweet, so as to be able to love it altogether : and all that I wish for others, or dare to recommend to them, is that they should keep their lives sweet also, not after my fashion, but each man in his own way. . . . Now I am sometimes blamed for not labouring more earnestly to bring down the good of which I prate into the lives of other men. My critics suppose, apparently, that I mean by the good some particular way of life or some type of character which is alone virtuous, and which ought to be propagated. Alas, their propagandas ! How they have filled this world with hatred, darkness, and blood ! How they are still the eternal obstacle, in every home and in every heart, to a simple happiness ! I have no wish to propagate any particular character, least of all my own ; my conceit does not take that form. I wish individuals, and races, and nations to be themselves, and to multiply the forms of perfection and happiness, as nature prompts them. The only thing which I think might be propagated without injustice to the types thereby suppressed is harmony ; enough harmony to prevent the interference of one type with another, and to allow the perfect development of each type. The good, as I conceive it, is happiness for each man after his own heart, and for each hour according to its inspiration. . . .

This is well said, though it is, of course, an over-statement ; the first part of it would suggest that he was depriving himself of any licence to criticize, and actually a good deal of his work, and that not the least valuable, consists of social criticism that is at once very acute and very decided ; whereas the little clause about " harmony " so quietly insinuated into the last part would suggest that he is also depriving himself of any license to enjoy, for what, we may ask, constitutes " harmony " when every type tends to interfere with every other, and what types are to be suppressed, and on what grounds. The sternest and narrowest moralist would ask for little more than this, if he were allowed to interpret " harmony " as he pleased. Nevertheless the statement will serve as a last link in the little chain of evidence that began with Mr. Santayana's cosmopolitanism and detachment ; and we can see now where he is.

His attitude is really an æsthetic one. Had he attended to nothing but his emotions and allowed them to well up into passionate rhythmical expression, he might have been a poet (he has written poetry), like Wordsworth ; had he passed his time observing the private life of men and women in society, he might have written novels, like Meredith ; had he chosen to brood perpetually over literature and art, he might have been a critic (as he is, of course, to some extent), like Pater ; but he has chosen the myths and allegories, the ideas and dreams of men as his subject, and them he weaves into many-coloured meditations and epics of gorgeous illusion that loom and glow and pass and fade like sunset clouds. With him, we feel that the details of expression, the crisp epigram that contrasts so felicitously two faiths or the magnificent piece of imagery that describes the mind under the sway of some philosophical idea, are not the means, of which the assertion of some underlying conviction is the end, but are rather the end themselves, and that the thesis, though by no means contemptible, is really only an excuse for their existence. The temperaments of most philosophers are writ large over their systems ; unconsciously they

indulge their leading characteristics and shape a
universe in which they themselves can move freely.
Even Mr. Bertrand Russell, who breathed for so long
the rarefied air of pure mathematics and only
descended from the heights of inviolate being to
give us his " logical atomism " and to express his
horror of humanistic systems, clearly takes pleasure
in the cold starlit universe he fashions and enjoys to
the full his stoic counsels of brave despair.   Mr.
Santayana has only indulged his temperament a little
more frankly.   Artist that he is, he is a spectator
content to lounge for ever in the playhouse of the
moon-coloured myths, the shifting allegories and
systems, the dance of ideas and dreams, bringing to
the show a delicate imagination and an easy sympathy
that is without a speck of passion, only occasionally
rising from his seat to hiss off some outrageous mystic
or rigid pompous idealist who has occupied the stage
too long.   There are books, he once told us, " in
which the footnotes, or the comments scrawled by
some reader's hand in the margin, are more interesting
than the text.   The world is one of these books."
But in this instance, we gather, the book is " real,"
while the footnotes and comments are only part of a
shifting dream. Only the Indian philosophers, meditat-
ing for decades in their savage and vivid jungles that
were nothing more to them than idle mist and smoke,
have travelled further along the path that leads to
the hollow land of illusion beyond illusion.   In
one place, Mr. Santayana very characteristically
exclaims :

It is this sorry self of mine sitting here in the dark, one in this serried pack of open-mouthed fools, hungry for illusion, that is responsible for the spectacle; for if a foolish instinct had not brought me to the playhouse, and if avid eyes and an idealizing understanding had not watched the performance, no part of it would have abused me: and if no one came to the theatre, the actors would soon flit away like ghosts, the poets would starve, the scenery would topple over and become rubbish, and the very walls would disappear. Every part of experience is illusion; and the source of this illusion is my animal nature, blindly labouring in a blind world. . . .

Once more the spectacle and the playhouse, Prospero before his ghostly revels.

There can be discovered in nearly all philosophical systems some hint as to what their ingenious creators consider to be the chief end of man, to which all the monstrous activities of Nature have so far pointed the way; and time and again the philosophers show their hands in this fashion; one will offer us a Prussian civil servant, another a reformer on the Town Council, another a professor and examiner, and so forth; and Mr. Santayana, himself a half-wistful, half-cynical spectator at the show of life, has with more than usual frankness produced a system that is at heart nothing but an elaborate defence or even glorification of the spectator's attitude. Behind his Life of Reason there stands, most plain to see, a company of comfortable, cultured, fairly sensitive, much-travelled and know-ledgeable gentlemen with fine prose styles. The Life of Reason, which is not only the title of his most ambitious performance, but is really the subject of everything he has written, is perhaps the best philosophical defence there has been of the æsthetic attitude. It demands some explanation. (Though it is high time I pointed out that to me, who am no philosopher, not even a thoroughgoing student of philosophy, but only a kind of literary critic with spasmodic and uncertain philosophical interests, all this is very dangerous ground.) What Mr. Santayana calls Reason, then, has two functions. In the name of Science, it investigates and reports upon that world of matter in which we, as animals, have our place ; everything that exists has its source in the world of matter, this physical universe ; which is not a creation of our own minds (though every interpretation of it is), which does not necessarily accommodate itself to our needs (though they will probably find satisfaction in what, after all, created them), and from which there is no appeal. The human consciousness is, of course, but one other product of matter, and we are, so to speak, kept going in such a world just as all its other creatures are kept going, by what Mr. Santayana has lately called our " animal faith." But Reason has another and greater task than to report this " real " world (greater because knowledge itself is, after all, a value), and that is to bring harmony into the ideal realm of values, which has a significance for us not possessed by the " real " world, if only because it is shaped by the special needs and preferences of our own particular nature. The two worlds are bridged by Mr. Santayana's system of " essences " which are what is perceived by consciousness and understood to be what has been called the " nature " of things, the first cousins of " sub-

stance " or the Platonic " idea." Out of such
" essences," of course, the Life of Reason builds up
its ideal realm in which we discover the ends of all
those things that have their root in our animal life.
Here, for example, is Mr. Santayana's account of love :

In popular feeling, where sentiment and observation must
both make themselves felt somehow or other, the tendency
is to imagine that love is an absolute, non-natural energy
which, for some unknown reason, or for none at all, lights upon
particular persons, and rests there eternally, as on its ultimate
goal. In other words, it makes the origin of love divine and
its object natural : which is the exact opposite of the truth.
If it were once seen, however, that every ideal expresses some
natural function, and that no natural function is incapable
in its free exercise, of evolving some ideal and finding justification, not in some collateral animal, but in an inherent operation
like life or thought, which being transmissible in its form is
also eternal, then the philosophy of love should not prove
permanently barren. For love is a brilliant illustration of a
principle everywhere discoverable : namely, that human
reason lives by turning the friction of material forces into the
light of ideal goods. There can be no philosophic interest in
disguising the animal basis of love, or in denying its spiritual
sublimations, since all life is animal in its origin and all spiritual
in its possible fruits.

There never was a better system for the purely contemplative mind, and even from this inadequate
account it can be seen how he has magnificently
indulged his temperament and, passing quickly over
the quagmires of metaphysics, has given himself per-
mission to wander at will over the hills and through
the jungles of human thought and dream :

The life of Reason, as I conceive it, is simply the dreaming
mind becoming coherent, devising symbols and methods, such

as languages, by which it may fitly survey its own career, and the forces of nature on which that career depends. Reason thereby raises our vegetative dream into a poetic revelation and transcript of the truth. . . .

And if, scuttling from Philosophy back to Literature, we regard him as a kind of artist in philosophic reverie, we can see now that many characteristics that so far have seemed to stand to his disadvantage really give him a great advantage over other persons in the same field, and make him what he undoubtedly is, a unique figure. Thus his cosmopolitan detachment enables him to survey the centuries and the nations without passion, and yet, not being a visitor from another planet, but simply a man who owes his ancestry and childhood to one race, his education to another, something of his culture, perhaps, to a third, and so on, he can claim some sort of kinship with many men and things and is able to brood over them with a sympathy that owes something to such kinship. Indeed, although he may appear to be all of a piece, those who read him closely may observe even yet certain warring elements that suggest that he has not yet completely harmonized the influences of two continents and two cultures ; thus, as one critic has pointed out, a tendency towards a certain prim and bloodless intellectuality competes in his mind with the artist's joyous acceptance of whatever is original and engrossing ; and we may say that in him the Spanish-American War is still languishing. But most readers, however, are more likely to complain of his consistency, the closeness and apparent sameness of his murmurous undulating text, than of his inconsistency, his failure to blend together indistinguishably the Spaniard and the American, the Catholic poet and the naturalistic philosopher, the professor and the artist.

His literary approach to his subject, his power as a stylist, however it may affect the schools, is all sheer gain to us, not merely because his style makes him so much more pleasant to read, but because his meditations and reveries are partly those of a poet, no matter what their subject-matter may be, for they describe states of mind and these can be more scrupulously pictured with the aid of bright images and cunning rhythms. His style runs back to an older kind of prose, the prose of men who, like him, loved the contemplative life, leisurely thought and vivid and quaint imagery, the prose of our seventeenth century. There is an echo of that old prose, perhaps not more than that; the differences are too great, and if they were any less Mr. Santayana would not be a writer with a fine personal style, but an archaic trifler, a philosopher at a literary fancy-dress ball. But we have only to remember that our ornate seventeenth-century prose took as its basis the paragraph and not the sentence, and substitute lighter stops for the modern writer's periods, and the likeness is plain. There is nothing deliberately archaic in the two following passages, and yet they make light of the intervening centuries:

To be born is painful, and the profit of it so uncertain that we need not wonder if sometimes the mind as well as the body seems to hold back. The winds of February are not

colder to a featherless chick than are the surprises which
nature and truth bring to our dreaming egotism . . .

or again :

There is an uncovenanted society of spirits, like that of the
morning stars singing together, or of all the larks at once in the
sky ; it is a happy accident of freedom and a conspiracy of
solitudes. When people talk together, they are at once
entangled in a mesh of instrumentalities, irrelevance, mis-
understanding, vanity, and propaganda ; and all to no purpose,
for why should creatures become alike who are different?
But when minds, being naturally akin and each alone in its
own heaven, soliloquize in harmony, saying compatible things
only because their hearts are similar, then society is a friendship
in the spirit ; and the unison of many thoughts twinkles
happily in the night across the void of separation. . . .

Both these passages are from the *Soliloquies in England,*
in which volume our author's style, reaching out to
all manner of subjects, is probably at its best. His
more ambitious work, the five volumes that compose
the *Life of Reason* and survey religion, philosophy,
art, and society, he has called " a presumptive
biography of the human intellect, which instead of
the Life of Reason might have been called the Romance
of Wisdom." But in truth, all that he has written
might very well carry both titles, for everything he
touches is so much coloured stuff for the loom on
which the Life of Reason is woven, and it is all a
soliloquy, a mind that the reader overhears recounting
all men's fables and old dreams. A philosopher, as
he has told us himself, is not necessarily every " logician
or psychologist who, in his official and studious
moments, may weigh argument against argument or

N

may devise expedients for solving theoretical puzzles " ; philosophy is a way of life, the contemplative attitude of mind ; and of philosophers in this sense, as distinct from the horde of official reasoners and speculators, the professors, and examiners, we have all too few ; such men have the poet's wonder, but it takes a different direction and overflows into wise reverie.

The reader who is himself something of a philosopher in this sense and who has been driven out of the well-trodden groves by the raving prophets, the shouting propagandists, the ceaseless noise of axes at the grindstone, will discover in this remoter grove, where the birds can still be heard singing in the trees, heaped treasures of thought. And he may take this body of work in one of two ways, or in both. He may regard it as so many essays on all manner of subjects, from Skylarks to the Irony of Liberalism, from Queen Mab to the British Hegelians, just as Mr. Logan Pearsall Smith has done in his admirable anthology of *Little Essays* selected from the works of Mr. Santayana ; or he may choose to follow Mr. Santayana's epic sweep and go wherever the Life of Reason bids him follow, and this will be the wiser choice, because then the epic note, the fullness of the vision, is not lost, and because some of Mr. Santayana's more gorgeous and elaborate traceries, such as the description of the ancient world, the rise of Catholicism and the advent of Protestantism in that great little history, *Reason in Religion* (*The Life of Reason*), must be read in full and in their place to be appreciated. But whatever the approach, the riches, imaginative, critical, historical, are there ; and in this endless reverie, woven so closely, with its slow undulating rhythm, there is almost everything that prose can offer, from gorgeous passages of description, image upon image, vista beyond vista, to witty epigrams as thick as October blackberries.   Flashes of wit light up every page ; we have only to dip into the volumes to bring out wise and witty sentences by the handful :

Popular poets are the parish priests of the Muse, retailing her ancient divinations to a long since converted public. . . .

Dickens entered the theatre of this world by the stage-door. . . .

Nothing is more pitiable than the attempts people make, who think they have an exquisite sensibility, to live in a house all of one period.   The connoisseur, like an uncritical philosopher, boasts to have patched his dwelling perfectly together, but he has forgotten himself, its egregious inhabitant. . . .

Nietzsche was far from ungenerous or unsympathetic towards the people.   He wished them (somewhat contemptuously) to be happy, whilst he and his superman remained poetically wretched. . . .

I do not profess to know what matter is in itself, and feel no confidence in the divination of those *esprits forts* who, leading a life of vice, thought the universe must be composed of nothing but dice and billiard-balls. . . .

The critic, feeling that something in the artist has escaped him, may labour to put himself in the artist's place.   If he succeeded, the result would only be to make him a biographer ; he would be describing in words the very intuitions which the artist had rendered in some other medium.   To understand how the artist felt, however, is not criticism ; criticism is an investigation of what the work is good for. . . .

Often the richest philosophies are the most sceptical; the mind is not then tethered in its home paddock, but ranges at will over the wilderness of being. The Indians, who deny the existence of the world, have keen sense for its infinity and its variegated colours; they play with the monstrous and miraculous in the grand manner, as in the *Arabian Nights*. No critic has had a sharper eye for the outline of ideas than Hume, who found it impossible to believe that they revealed anything. . . .

The extent to which æsthetic values are allowed to colour the resultant or highest good is a point of great theoretic importance, not only for art, but for general philosophy. If art is excluded altogether or given only a trivial rôle, perhaps as a necessary relaxation, we feel at once that a philosophy so judging human arts is ascetic or post-rational. It pretends to guide life from above and from without; it has discredited human nature and mortal interests, and has thereby undermined itself, since it is at best but a partial expression of that humanity which it strives to transcend. If, on the contrary, art is prized as something supreme and irresponsible, if the poetic and mystic glow which it may bring seems its own complete justification, then philosophy is evidently still pre-rational, or, rather, non-existent; for the beasts that listened to Orpheus belong to this school. To be bewitched is not to be saved, though all the magicians and æsthetes in the world should pronounce it to be so. Intoxication is a sad business, at least for a philosopher; for you must either drown yourself altogether, or else when sober again you will feel somewhat fooled by yesterday's joys and somewhat lost in to-day's vacancy. The man who would emancipate art from discipline and reason is trying to elude rationality, not merely in art, but in all existence. He is vexed at conditions of excellence that make him conscious of his own incompetence and failure. Rather than consider his function, he proclaims his self-sufficiency. A way foolishness has of revenging itself is to excommunicate the world. . . .

We all know that enthusiastic, excellent but occasionally irritating friend who keeps us from our gossip while he reads out passage after passage from the book he has last read and admired.   There are limits beyond which even the critic, with his licence to quote, should not go, and unfortunately I have already passed those limits, although Mr. Santayana's volumes on the table still bristle with slips that mark quotations illustrating half a dozen different characteristics.   There is perhaps no better proof of a writer's ability to wed together clear-pointed thought and sharply etched expression than this desire to quote on and on, brushing aside any suggestions of paraphrase or mere comment.   In an age that turns aside from contemplation and wise reverie, an age that delights in bludgeoning the nearest passer-by with the first idea it comes upon, Mr. Santayana, even without his wit and style, would still be a notable figure by reason of his wide knowledge, rich imagination, and contemplative attitude, telling over the innumerable signs and symbols of the world.   Fortunately, the wit and the style are there, too, and he is more than notable, he is a unique figure :

Voyaging through strange seas of Thought, alone . . .

and returning to heap the treasure at our feet.

THE POETRY OF MR. J. C. SQUIRE

THE position of Mr. J. C. Squire in contemporary poetry is very curious. Traditionalists and persons who have a horror of innovation in poetry have regarded him as a dangerous rebel, a man out to destroy the ease and comeliness, the old beauty of our verse; whereas, on the other hand, the wild young men, who believe that poetry was born again when they first set down their obscure reactions in jerky prose, have seen in Mr. Squire a mere slave of empty tradition and have suggested that he can hardly be considered a poet at all. Further, not being a member of any school or group (for the so-called " Georgians," about whom there has been far too much talk, are not really a school or group) and not being easy to " place," he has been rather neglected by those critics who have written little books on modern verse, its tendencies, its revolt, its Vision and Idealism, its want of Vision and Idealism; he has been left to himself. Yet he has been consistently enjoyed and praised by persons who take the poetry of their own time seriously and examine it curiously in their search for original minds and fine craftsmen, and such persons have looked forward to every succeeding volume of work that Mr. Squire has given them, secure in the knowledge that in him they had discovered both an original mind and a fine craftsman. Actually, the explanation of this curious position of his lies in the fact that he is original, one of the most original poets we have ; the rigid conservatives and the wild rebels have both assailed him simply because he is in neither of their camps ; he is in his own camp ; he has done what every original poet has always done, he has not broken away from tradition, but he has modified it to suit his own purposes. He is an experimenter, and, as I shall presently endeavour to prove, a successful experimenter. Having new matter to his hand, he has fashioned new and fit forms in order that such matter might be expressed scrupulously. Many poets are content, and rightly content, to take the traditional measures and bring them as near to absolute perfection as it is possible for mortal man ; they sing the old songs and are happy in doing nothing beyond lengthening a pause and remodelling a cadenza ; the wine they bring is like that of their father's and grandfather's vintaging, and so they pour it into the same delicate old beakers ; and such poets are commonly exquisite craftsmen, but they have not original minds ; they have not enlarged the scope of poetry ; they do not conquer, for poetry's sake, some new territory of the human mind. But an original poet, if he is to be successful as a poet and not merely as an " original," has to enlarge the scope of his art, has to take the traditional practices of his craft and bend and twist them to fit his own mind, so that in the end he has both personal things to say and a personal manner of saying them; and this means that, his task accomplished, the art of poetry is not what it was three hundred years before he was born, for it is, as it were, wearing a collar and tie instead of a ruff; and yet, because of these changes, the art of poetry really is, in its essence, what it was three hundred years before, simply because it serves the human creature with a collar and tie precisely as it served the human creature with a ruff. An art is like Alice in the Looking-Glass Wood, it has to run in order to keep in the same place. But while an original artist will have to modify tradition in order to express himself properly, he is not asked to depart altogether from tradition, to begin, in fact, a new one; to do this with any chance of success argues a degree of originality, a godlike superiority to whole generations of fellow-creatures, only to be met with once or twice in a thousand years. Moreover, no artist should break away from tradition at all and fashion new forms until he knows the tradition and the old forms and is sure that they will not serve his turn. All the great artistic rebels have shown a sound working knowledge of the older forms against which they have protested. If a man is convinced that forms once glorious and significant have now declined into mechanical shifts and empty devices, the props and stays of dull minds, he can cast them off, but he must first make sure what it is he is pruning away, he must know them by heart, these tricks of the trade.

This phrase brings us sharply back to Mr. Squire,

who has amused literary England with a book of parodies bearing that title. In this and other well-known volumes he has shown expert knowledge of the " tricks of the trade " ; he has parodied many contemporary writers ; he has made famous poets of different periods write each other's works, a kind of *pastiche* rather than parody ; and he has written a number of capital burlesques of certain popular kinds of prose and verse ; and in all these activities he has shown great skill and humour, and, what is important, a very critical appreciation of a large number of common literary tendencies and stock devices. A typical example of his manner can be found in his burlesque of a sonnet in the grand style, a sonnet that can form (and has formed) the basis of a rather malicious experiment, which consists of reading it aloud to a company of fairly poetical persons, not in the secret, and then asking for an opinion of its value :

No purple mars the chalice ; not a bird
　Shrills o'er the solemn silence of thy fame.
　No echo of the mist that knows no name
Dims the fierce darkness of the odorous word.
The shadowy sails of all the world are stirred,
　The pomps of hell go down in utter flame,
　And never a magic master stands to shame
The hollow of the hill the Titan heard.

O move not, cease not, heart ! Time's acolyte
　Frustrates forlorn the windows of the west
　And beats the blinding of our bitter tears,
Immune in isolation ; whilst the night
　Smites with her stark immortal palimpsest
　The green arcades of immemorial years !

A good parodist, and Mr. Squire has proved himself one of the best parodists we have, needs something more than a sense of the ludicrous and a nodding acquaintance with a number of different literary styles ; he has to have an eye for the superficialities, the empty gestures, the pompous nothings, the mechanical tricks, the insincerities, that are present even in good work ; and though a parodist may often handle an author whom he admires, the characteristics which he fastens upon and exaggerates are practically always the least admirable characteristics, the spots in the sun. The moment when the great author loses his grasp, yawns, and proceeds lazily to imitate himself, is the moment when the parodist swoops down and captures his prey. It is clearly important, then, to recollect that at the time when Mr. Squire was forming his own manner in verse, he was also parodying other men's manners and doing it with almost devastating skill ; Mr. Squire the poet, we may say, had to work with one eye upon Mr. Squire the parodist. Small wonder then that we discover in this poetry, almost in its earliest form, an austerity, a determination to beat out the matter honestly and sincerely, a freedom from all cheap devices, on the part of its author. Indeed, in the earlier work, there is clearly something laboured, something struggling to free itself and not quite succeeding, and this only passes as the poet perfects his own manner. This, it must be understood, was obviously his only real difficulty. In matters of ordinary " technique," the handling of metrical speech, the business of rhyming,

and so forth, Mr. Squire was almost from the first
accomplished, even brilliant ; there are probably
very few men writing who could compose a light,
witty, satirical piece, say, a ballade, so deftly and
quickly as he can. He is one of the few poets of the
last two generations who have given us a volume of
satirical verse. *The Survival of the Fittest : And
Other Poems*, which was published in 1916 and reprinted three times during the same year, is a little
book of ironical ballads and epigrams, for the most
part on topical themes connected with the war, and
nothing better of its kind has been done in our time.
The manner of these things is easy, almost casual,
and without the usual straining that seems to attend
most of our present attempts to use verse as a medium
for satire ; but this casual manner is only a light cloak
for the poet's merciless wit and his almost savage
determination to make every shot hit the bull's-eye.
Liberalism never had a better sharp-shooter. Such
verses as *The Dilemma :*

> God heard the embattled nations sing and shout
> " Gott strafe England ! " and " God save the King ! "
> God this, God that, and God the other thing—
> " Good God ! " said God, " I've got my work cut out."

seem as casual as a remark made in a dressing-
room, and yet are as effective as a bursting bomb.
But the whole book, with its unusual combination
of ease and point, is effective, and is an excellent
example of its writer's mastery of the lighter tools
of his craft.

His poetry proper is now contained in three volumes.

The first, *Poems : First Series*, gives us a selection, all that the poet wishes to retain, from four earlier and smaller books of verse, together with a certain number of new poems. Fortunately, he has dated every poem, so that we can easily follow the progress of his art, from the earliest contribution, in 1905, to the group written in 1917. The second volume, *Poems : Second Series*, includes everything he wrote of any importance in verse during the years 1918–1921. The last book, *American Poems and Others*, is the work of 1921–1922, with the exception of one poem, *The World* 1918. Here, then, is a body of work, about a hundred poems, some of them of considerable length, that after much winnowing, and, we may guess, much trial and experiment and ruthless destruction, remains a considerable canon, and represents twenty years of the labour and delight of one of the most brilliant men of letters of the time, who has shown himself, as we have seen, to be a searching and fastidious critic of the art of poetry, who has studied its history and its masters, who knows all its shifts and devices, who has turned to many different kinds of work and been astonishingly successful in most of them, but who has really given his best energies to the creation of his poetry and has there fully revealed his personality, his doubt and wonder and delight. It is fortunate for us that he did not prune away all his early work, for the few early poems at the beginning of *Poems : First Series* show us a man struggling towards self-expression, that is, the expression of an original personality in an original form, rather

than a man who has early attained self-expression ;
we see here a poet who has a great deal of very unusual
matter to give form to, and is still restlessly experi-
menting in the hope of finding forms that are suited
to it. Mr. Lynd has said, very wisely, of Mr. Squire
that " He beats out a music of his own and he beats
out an imagery of his own," and in this early work we
can watch the beating. The metaphor is a good one
if only because it suggests effort, and Mr. Squire is
a poet who has never relaxed from effort and it is
clear that his Muse at first suffered from the birth-
pangs and never, or rarely ever, had easy deliveries.
Being so impressionable, he must have caught himself
echoing the music of other men. Even here, after
the winnowing, there is, for example, more than one
suggestion of our old friend, the *Shropshire Lad :*

> Dark fir-tops foot the moony sky,
>   Blue Moonlight bars the drive ;
> Here at the open window I
>   Sit smoking and alive.

Here and there he shows his ingenuity in uncommon
measures, and though he is not a metrical genius, in
places he has taken hold of elaborate traditional
forms and made exquisite use of them. There is one
little song of his, *Behind the Lines,* a little piece of
chain verse, an elaborate variation of the *pantoum,*
which is as ingenious as anything Clement Marot
himself ever wrote, and is much nearer fine poetry
than most of the similar experiments by the Dobson-
Lang school :

The wind of evening cried along the darkening trees,
Along the darkening trees, heavy with ancient pain,
Heavy with ancient pain from faded centuries,
From faded centuries. . . . O foolish thought and vain !

O foolish thought and vain to think the wind could know,
To think the wind could know the griefs of men who died,
The griefs of men who died and mouldered long ago :
" And mouldered long ago," the wind of evening cried.

But already he had reached the height of his success
in the experiments with traditional forms (I am
leaving out of sight his own special modification of
the form, the one that is peculiarly his own, to which
I shall return below) in *The Lily of Malud,* that piece
of romantic anthropology which lies outside the
general drift of Mr. Squire's work and is really a
terrific *tour de force*. The poem itself is like its own
subject, a strange and beautiful flower born of mud.
It is very finely imagined, but it is chiefly a triumph
of technique ; its curious muttering closeness and
its criss-cross of rhymes give it the very atmosphere of some aboriginal sacred dance, with the
soft tom-toms going, the grunting of the dancers,
the swishing and thudding of their naked bodies ;
it rises and falls like a ceremonial dance, beginning
very quietly, but with an inevitable swaying
movement :

The lily of Malud is born in secret mud.
It is breathed like a word in a little dark ravine
Where no bird was ever heard and no beast was ever seen,
And the leaves are never stirred by the panther's velvet
    sheen.

and rising to a climax of excitement :

> O it moved as it grew !
> It is moving, opening, with calm and gradual will,
> And their bodies where they cling are shadowed and still
> And with marvel they mark that the mud now is dark
> For the unfolding flower, like a goddess in her power,
> Challenges the moon with a light of her own,
> That lovelily grows as the petals unclose,
> Wider, more wide with an awful inward pride,
> Till the heart of it breaks, and stilled is their breath,
> For the radiance it makes is as wonderful as death . . .

and then, at the end, sinking away into nothing but
the beat of tom-toms in the memory :

> Something sorrowful and far, something sweet and vaguely
>   seen
> Like an early evening star when the sky is pale green :
> A quiet silver tower that climbed in an hour,
> Or a ghost like a flower, or a flower like a queen :
> Something holy in the past that came but did not last . . .

But it is clear from the early poems that what we may
call his really characteristic modes of thought, his
curious reveries and introspection, his philosophic
imagination, linking some fleeting thought or emotion
with wide sweeps of time and space, have not yet
found their proper modes of expression. Such poems
as *Antinomies on a Railway Station, The Mind of Man,
Ode : In a Restaurant* are bringing something new
into poetry, but, good as they are, their thought is
still awkward and uncomfortable in clothes that do
not quite fit. The poet's manner has not yet been
perfected, and as yet he cannot rise from a casual
colloquialism to some image of Beauty or Death and

sink back again without any obvious change of key. Thus, in the Ode, just before he gives us such a curious and satisfying image as this :

> The sounds pierce in and die again,
> Like keen-drawn threads of ink dropped into a glass
> Of water, which curl and relax and soften and pass . . .

he can still give us a quatrain of this kind :

> How horrible this noise ! this air how thick !
> It is disgusting. . . . I feel sick . . .
> Loosely I prod the table with a fork,
> My mind gapes, dizzies, ceases to work . . .

in which we feel that he is a little too anxious to impress upon us the fact that his mind has ceased to work. Yet before we have turned over half the pages in this first volume, we have discovered definite signs of a personal note and a personal form ; and in the second half of this volume and in the two later ones, they are present unmistakably and are gathering strength almost with every succeeding poem.

Mr. Squire has written lyrics in more or less elaborate measures, he has used blank verse, heroic couplets, and various stanza forms with various rhyme schemes, he has made experiments in free verse ; but in all his best, his really characteristic, work, he has attempted to keep as close to the traditional usages as he could while loosening and, as it were, " flattening " the cadence of the verse, so that it has the movement of talk (and, of course, in particular, his own talk) and yet preserves the stress, the pattern, though not the cramped patterns of some older kinds, of poetry.

Many poets have tried to make their lines seem as
natural as speech, and some few have succeeded,
notably Mr. Yeats in his later work. But though
Mr. Yeats may give us poetry that is like somebody's
speech, nevertheless it is not our speech, that of
ordinary educated Englishmen living in the early
twentieth century, not merely because it does not
employ our colloquialisms, but also because its cadence
is very different. Now Mr. Squire, having curious,
original matter to express, having to hand certain
thoughts and emotions that are at once intimately
personal and yet very general, expressing the age,
has chosen a manner that is peculiarly fitting, for it
has the cadence of the speech we know, the familiar
music that we hear every day in talk, but it is cunningly heightened, and is so elastic that it can rise
from something deliberately commonplace, banal,
from the air of the Underground Railway, to an
image that is a triumph of the philosophic imagination, to an eagle's height, and can do all this without
breaking the continuity of the poetry and making
the style look like a Neapolitan ice. Because this
manner is so apparently natural, so familiar, it is
particularly fitted for what we might call the poetry
of reverie ; and because it is so elastic, having so
wide a scope when cunningly used, it lends itself to
dramatic effects ; and so it happens that Mr. Squire
is unusually successful in a kind of poetry that may
be called dramatic reverie. There is, for example,
the *Meditation in Lamplight*, in which he first broods
over death :

o

What deaths men have died, not fighting but impotent.
Hung on the wire, between trenches, burning and freezing,
Groaning for water with armies of men so near ;
The fall over cliff, the clutch at the rootless grass,
The beach rushing up, the whirling, the turning head first ;
Stiff writhings of strychnine, taken in error or haste,
Angina pectoris, shudders of the heart. . . .

and so forth, until, like most sensitive men at some
time or other, he cries to God to pity him and make
tolerable his end, or at least give him courage to die
manfully :

That I shrink not nor scream, gripped by the jaws of the
  vice ;
For the thought of it turns me sick, and my heart stands still,
Knocks and stands still.   O fearful, fearful Shadow,
Kill me, let me die to escape the terror of thee !

And then suddenly, at the beginning of the next
verse, the style sinks down into quiet ordinary speech :

A tap. Come in ! Oh, no, I am perfectly well,
Only a little tired. Take this one, it's softer.
How are things going with you ? Will you have some coffee ?
Well, of course it's trying sometimes, but never mind,
It will probably be all right.   Carry on, and keep cheerful,
I shouldn't, if I were you, meet trouble half-way,
It is always best to take everything as it comes.

And how else could this pitiful, ironical little drama
have been staged in words ? Or, for another example,
there is the quieter piece in the earlier volume, *August
Moon*, which dates from the later years of the war.
It begins with an exquisitely subdued picture of a
quiet summer evening, the kind of description in

which Mr. Squire excels ; we see the calm river and
the calm sky :

Silence.   Time is suspended ; that the light falls
One would not know were it not for the moon in the sky ;
And the broken moon in the water, whose fractures tell
Of slow broad ripples that otherwise do not show,
Maturing imperceptibly from a pale to a deeper gold,
A golden half moon in the sky, and broken gold in the water.

In the water, tranquilly severing, joining, gold :
Three or four little plates of gold on the river :
A little motion of gold between the dark images
Of two tall posts that stand in the grey water.

There are voices passing, a murmur of quiet voices,
A woman's laugh, and children going home.
A whispering couple, leaning over the railings,
And, somewhere, a little splash as a dog goes in.

I have always known all this, it has always been,
There is no change anywhere, nothing will ever change.

I heard a story, a crazy and tiresome myth.

Listen ! behind the twilight a deep low sound
Like the constant shutting of very distant doors.

Doors that are letting people over there
Out to some other place beyond the end of the sky.

Here we have the atmosphere, the slow continuity, of
reverie, and yet here too the colossal insanity, the
awful intrusion, of war has never been more effectively
dramatized ; instead of describing how he saw this
and thought that, the poet puts his mind itself on
the stage, and actually it is only this personal style

of his that enables him to do it with such success. The deliberate introduction of colloquialisms, of flat commonplaces, of occasionally even banal adjectives, such as "that otherwise do not show" and the "tiresome" above, has probably left a good many readers, particularly those who are fond of their old poets, either puzzled or resentful, and they have probably accused Mr. Squire either of writing carelessly and badly or of being an impudent Realist, out to shock the conservative reader and half-contemptuous of the art he practises. Nothing, of course, could be further from the truth; in those poems where he aims at a heightened kind of talk, where not only the cadence of his lines is based on that of common speech, but the style may descend now and again into its very banalities, if he fails, he fails obviously, whereas, on the other hand, if he succeeds, his manner is so natural, so casual even, that his skill will pass unnoticed and once more art will have concealed art. Needless to say, sometimes he does fail, not only in words or phrases, but perhaps in whole poems, as we shall presently see.

Mr. Squire's characteristic art may be discovered, in one of its simplest and most effective forms, in what is perhaps his best-known poem, *To a Bull-Dog*, which is nothing more nor less than an elegy upon the death of a friend in the war. Scores of poets, some of them very good poets, wrote elegies during the war, but none of them produced anything so moving as this poem of Mr. Squire's; so that it is worth examining not only because it is a good and com-

paratively simple example of the way in which he
goes to work, but also because it is a poem in which
he treated a common subject more successfully than
most of his fellow-poets. The situation he handles
is really a complex of several equally poignant situations. The poet has lost his friend and the bull-dog
has lost its master, and the poet knows and the dog
does not know, and there seems to be no way of telling
a dog that Death has come trampling in, and before
the wistful gaze of this innocent and affectionate
brute the world of men with its unmeaning strife
and slaughter is hardly something to point to with
pride. Here, then, is material that, poetically considered, is at once as effective and as dangerous as
dynamite. If it is decorated, all frilled and starched
with imagery and fine phrases, it will inevitably be
frigid, the record of a stuffed bull-dog, a frozen
poet and a friend who could never have been anything else but dead ; but if decoration can kill the
poem, so can an excess of sentiment, or rather, sentiment that has become aware of itself and become
sentimentality, for the situation is one that could
dynamite the emotions and is clearly a fat and greasy
find for the sentimentalist. Mr. Squire, with nice
tact, avoids both these dangers ; the poem he writes
is not decorated and makes use of none of those
poetical devices that give a subject a superficial
richness and significance ; it does not daub the lily ;
nor, on the other hand, does it unworthily assault the
emotions and give us any " droppings of warm tears."
The poet makes it apparently as simple and casual as

talk, but talk that has a very natural but very moving cadence, and the result is a little poem that is clean and fresh, with the dignity that a man's real sorrow takes to itself, and yet, as we have seen, is more poignant than any of the hundred and one poems of lamentation that the war has brought forth. Here, for the benefit of those who do not remember the poem or who have never read it, are the last few verses, though the whole poem should be read in the light of this criticism :

When summer comes again,
    And the long sunsets fade,
We shall have to go on playing the feeble game for two
    That since the war we've played.

And though you run expectant as you always do
    To the uniforms we meet,
You'll never find Willy among all the soldiers
    In even the longest street,

Nor in any crowd ; yet, strange and bitter thought,
    Even now were the old words said,
If I tried the old trick and said, " Where's Willy ? "
    You would quiver and lift your head,

And your brown eyes would look to ask if I were serious,
    And wait for the word to spring.
Sleep undisturbed : I shan't say *that* again,
    You innocent old thing.

I must sit, not speaking, on the sofa,
    While you lie asleep on the floor ;
For he's suffered a thing that dogs couldn't dream of,
    And he won't be coming here any more.

You have only to talk the poem and you are singing it, you cannot sing it without talking it ; it is quiet conversation moving to a heart-breaking melody. The rhyme scheme is just right for its purpose ; had all four lines been rhymed, it would have been somewhat too tight, and its casual air would have disappeared ; had there been no rhymes at all, the song would have been lost in the talk without the little chime of the second and fourth lines. It is characteristic of the poet's quiet audacity that at the emotional height of the poem, in the last verse but one, he should become more colloquial than ever, and even make use of the italicized " that " and allow his own and the reader's emotion to find relief in the sudden, " You innocent old thing," just as women find relief for their emotions in such phrases. The structure of the poem seems to demand such a verse, but I am not sure that it compensates for a certain loss of dignity and austerity that the manner, despite its casual air, achieves everywhere else in the poem.

A genuine poet cannot be original in manner without being original in mind, and so far we have seen more of Mr. Squire's manner than his mind. I have said already that he has brought something new into poetry, and it still remains to be seen what that something is. The characteristics he shares with most other poets worth talking about can be noticed in passing. He has a very strong visualizing imagination, and is particularly happy with pieces of description in a very quiet tone, coloured dimly by the poet's mood of reverie. He has, too, an unusually fine power of close observation, not only, like the well-trained journalist, of the telling details of the outward scene, but also of his own mind in conjunction with the outward scene, his own mental reactions. That long and very powerful poem, *The Stockyard*, in the *American Poems*, the result of nothing more than a hasty visit to a stockyard, is a magnificent example of this power, an enormous *tour de force*. Picture after picture, vivid in the light of the poet's horror, is flashed past our eyes :

A sound of perpetual scraping, a warm wet stench . . .
And then, still steaming, moved evenly into a hall
A line of pinkish-white pigs, atrociously naked,
Their unders gashed with a wound from tail to head,
Suspended parallel, a quivering pattern of trunks
And dangling snouts and smooth flapping pointed ears,
A shifting geometrical maze of bodies
That trembled when turning the corners. . . .

Or again :

In a narrow high passage, half hogs came tumbling outward
To the top of an inclined plane of wood, slid down
And stuck at the base a second to be smitten in two.
A dark young man with an axe was standing there,
Lean-waisted, strong-armed ; one fancied a mask like a heads-
    man's.
He waited, axe downwards, his eyes looking at us and through
    us,
His mouth was firm, chin square, he'd a slight dark moustache :
Slavonic perhaps. There was pride and contempt in his eyes,
And nothing else lived in his face to show what he thought.
A carcass rushed down ; his hands went steadily upwards,
Then down flew the axe and severed it clean between bones,

To tumble down funnels . . . I answered ashamed his gaze
As he stood, imperious, erect, his eyes looking forward,
Axe at rest, straight down from his forearm, a waiting headsman,
A figure from allegory, a symbol of Doom.

The man and the scene have been caught and fixed
for ever. And because an unusual power of observation has here been placed at the service of strong
emotions, the resulting poem is more powerful than
half a dozen realistic novels on the same theme. In
an admirable lecture on Subject in Poetry, Mr. Squire
himself has pointed out that only those objects should
come into a poem which have associated themselves
with the poet's emotion, and if he had chosen to do
so he could have taken some excellent examples from
his own poetry, which happens to be a poetry that is
continually taking in new objects that have become
associated in some way with the poet's emotions. He
could, too, it seems to me, have taken some bad
examples, in which the poet's power of observation
appears to have been working independently of his
feelings and he himself appears to have been coldly
taking notes. Thus, the *Rugger Match*, though it
grapples with a tough poetical subject does not
grapple with one so tough as that in *The Stockyard*;
and yet it is certainly an inferior piece of work,
partly because its semi-philosophical conclusion seems
forced, almost like a parody of the poet's characteristic manner, and partly, too, because its detailed
pieces of description are not fused together, but have
an irritatingly independent existence ; so that though
the poem is very skilfully put together and has con-

siderable power, it does not ring quite true. Consider the opening lines :

The walls make a funnel, packed full ; the distant gate
Bars us from inaccessible light and peace.
Far over necks and ears and hats, I see
Policemen's helmets and cards hung on the ironwork :
" One shilling," " No change given," " Ticket-holders only " ;
Oh Lord ! What an awful crush ! There are faces pale
And strained, and faces with animal grins advancing,
Stuck fast round mine. We move, we pause again
For an age, then a forward wave and another stop.
The pressure might squeeze one flat. Dig heels into ground
For this white and terrified woman whose male insists
Upon room to get back. Why didn't I come here at one ?
Why come here at all ? What strange little creatures we are,
Wedged and shoving under the contemptuous sky !

There are too many moods and too many voices here ; and this weakness runs through the whole poem ; it is a thought too cool and clever, too " made," for poetry. But for this one failure, where the poet's power of observation has outstripped his emotions, there are a score of successes, all in subjects that invite disaster, but proclaim a triumph for the poetic genius that masters them. Mr. Squire's sense of words, that perception of the suggestive power of language, its super-meaning, which is one of the signs of the poetic mind, is not so astonishing as his power of observation ; it is sound and painstaking (improving with time) rather than " magical," as it is with some poets, who conjure epithets out of Paradise. When his really powerful imagination is firmly seated in the saddle (as it is, for example, in such poems as *Under* and *The Journey*, both of them surprisingly different from the main body of his work and both of them magically vivid), he can take anything in his stride; the poems, no matter how unpromising the material may seem, flower into lovely and appropriate images, and phrases and epithets of genius light up the verse. But if he is working, let us say, a little coldly, and working where so many other poets have gone before him, we do not discover him at his best. Thus, *The Moon*, has great merit; it is packed with vivid imagery, for which the ages have been plundered; it has an admirable stanza form; but nevertheless no one who really understood its author's genius would include it among his major works. It hardly lives up to its fine opening:

> I waited for a miracle to-night. . . .

for the reader, in the half-impudent, half-wistful manner of his kind, waits, too, for a miracle and is given instead some distinguished verse. Whereas, in some other things, the reader finds himself gently taken by the buttonhole and expects nothing but some commonplace matter, and yet discovers before he has done that he is seeing the mind of man against the background of eternity, and that the quiet button-holing poet is winged with great words.

This brings us to the end of Mr. Squire's comparative weaknesses and to the threshold of his strength; he is, above all the other writers of his generation, the poet of the philosophic imagination. Roughly speaking, without any intention of making an excursion into æsthetics, we may say that poetry and philosophy come together in three different ways. First, there are philosophers who have a poetic cast of mind and may record their experiences in verse, just as Mr. Santayana, who may be regarded as a member of this group, has done. Then there are poet-philosophers, whose work is poetry, probably great poetry, and yet is avowedly the vehicle of a more or less definite philosophy, sufficiently marked to entitle them to a place in any thorough history of thought. Wordsworth is, of course, the type. Then, lastly, there are poets who have hardly a philosophy, but have a philosophical cast of mind, who are continually brooding over appearance and reality, Time and change ; and among such poets Mr. Squire must be given a prominent place. He writes for the Hamlets and Prosperos of his time. Though making no pretence of having interests different from those of the common man, though apparently having a very full outward life and writing often of things of the moment, the greater part of his mind is in reality detached, turning and examining itself or roaming through Space and Time, relating some tiny fragment of personal experience to the whole history of the race. In his earlier poems, he is a taut and half-bitter realist, noting the delusiveness of appearance :

> What is this power that comes to my sight
> That I see a night without the night,
> That I see them clear, yet look them through,
> The silvery things and the darkly blue,

> That the solid wall seems soft as death,
>   A wavering and unanchored wraith,
> And rails that shine and stones that stream
>   Unsubstantial as a dream ?

and often exclaiming in disgusted wonder at life :

> Soul ! this life is very strange,
> And circumstances very foul
> Attend the belly's stormy howl. . . .

In the later poems, the wonder is there, but it is more romantic and exalted, as in that exquisite poem, *A Dog's Death* :

> . . . . It is strange how we buy our sorrow
> For the touch of perishing things, idly, with open eyes ;
> How we give our hearts to brutes that will die in a few seasons,
> Nor trouble what we do when we do it ; nor would have it
>   otherwise.

and also in many of the poems in the last volume, notably *The World :* 1918, *A London Sunset*, and that curiously fascinating record of two lovers, *Another Generation*, which crams half a lifetime into a few verses and yet is as human and concrete as the last good love-story. If, like most poets, he sings in a mood of regret and laments the passing of a person, a familiar scene, an experience, more often than not he comes to Change itself at last, though it may be only change in his own mind, as when he remembers, in Wordsworthian fashion, what beauty he saw about him when the earth was new, and regrets the change in himself :

> But now I walk this earth as it were a lumber room,
> And sometimes live a week, seeing nothing but mere herbs,
> Mere stones, mere passing birds . . .

and even better, when he speaks for a whole generation, the generation whose lives were split in two by
the war, and says something so finely that it has been
said now once for all :

> But now all memory
> Is one ironic truth,
> We look like strangers at the boys
> We were so long ago.
>
> For half of us are dead,
> And half have lost their youth,
> And our hearts are scarred by many griefs,
> That only age should know.

He has the philosopher's passionate interest in the
mind itself, and time and again he turns to it, as in
The Mind of Man, with its curious symbolism :

> Beneath my skull-bone and my hair,
> Covered like a poisonous well,
> There is a land : if you looked there
> What you saw you'd quail to tell . . .

and so on to the strange landscapes of this land, an
odd attractive poem ; and later, as in those poems in
which he describes, very truthfully under the cover
of picturesque imagery, poetic creation itself, such as
Prologue ; In Darkness and *Processes of Thought*, with
its Whitmanish gusto :

> Into the pit of my heart and brain
> My eyes, ears, nose, tongue, fingers, like five gardeners
> Are shovelling sights, sounds, odours, savours, contacts,
> While I, their master, casually nod. . . .

Such introspection and quaint imagery take us back
to Donne and the metaphysicals of the seventeenth

century. He will not only relate some fleeting
experience and emotion to a great historical background, he will also work in the opposite direction
and range through Space and Time to arrive at last
at some emotion or thought at the back of his mind.
In *Rivers,* he surveys in imagination the great European
rivers he has seen, then pushes forward to dream of
the great rivers of the world, to exclaim in a geo-
graphical ecstasy at the beauty and wonder of these
things, only to discover that :

> There is something still in the back of my mind
>   From very far away ;
> There is something I saw and see not,
> A country full of rivers
> That stirs in my heart and speaks to me
>   More sure, more dear than they . . .

and he suddenly remembers the little rivers of Devon,
the " lost country " of his boyhood, so that an
emotion common to all poets comes to us from a new
direction, curiously linked up with all manner of
thoughts, and so takes on a new significance. How
many English poets have written about birds—yet
this poet, in his *Birds,* gives us something new ;
beginning boldly :

> Within mankind's duration, so they say,
> Khephren and Ninus lived but yesterday

he takes us soaring through Time :

> O let your strong imagination turn
> The great wheel backward, until Troy unburn,
> And then unbuild, and seven Troys below
> Rise out of death, and dwindle and outflow,
> Till all have passed, and none has yet been there :
> Back, ever back . . .

(the very process stirs an unusual note of ecstasy in him) until we have seen the birds from the beginning of things and noted all their history in a flash and discovered how they have outwinged Change :

> O delicate chain over all the ages stretched,
> O dumb tradition from what far darkness fetched :
> Each little architect with its one design
> Perpetual, fixed and right in stuff and line,
> Each little ministrant who knows one thing,
> One learned rite to celebrate the spring.
> Whatever alters else on sea or shore,
> These are unchanging : man must still explore.

There is almost all of the poet's mind, from its wonder at Change, its historical attitude, its passion for the race, down to its interest in architecture, in this one verse. He cannot describe the delicate beauty of the environs of Washington without conjuring up the background of the ages :

> It seems unreal : a world of youth,
> So new and innocently gay,
> The mind will scarce accept the truth
> This land was not made yesterday,
> That through those years of Asia's kings
> Or ever Greece was glorified,
> Here also flowered all the springs,
> Here all the autumns burned and died . . .

and cannot pass Niagara without wondering whether the day will come again when it will roar unceasingly in a wilderness with nothing but the wild beasts to hear it. And, lastly, like most philosophical poets, he has risen to his greatest height as a phrase-maker when he has had to find an image for the brevity of man's life, for which so many memorable images have been found :

> . . . I see myself as one of a heap of stones
> Wetted a moment to life as the flying wave goes over.

And that will serve as an envoi from one of the most original poets of our time ; a brilliant journalist, apparently enmeshed in the affairs of to-day, and yet a dreamer, a detached mind, for ever roaming through the yesterdays and to-morrows ; one who is seemingly reserved, somewhat casual, and yet who has at times uncovered his mind and heart with almost savage sincerity ; a man who, amidst great difficulties, has never loosened his grip upon his art since he first went to it, and who has contrived to express both himself and his age in poetry that is new and strange only in the sense that all good art is new and strange—for a day, and then, like all good art, will be half-strange, half-familiar, and altogether beautiful and satisfying for generations.

Date Due
